"The idea of a 10-minute Java Break is a very doable concept and will fulfill our need to spend time each day with the Lord, and yet not be overwhelmed by the time crunch. It's the perfect solution that will provide us with inner peace and restore our souls. Thank you, Anne, for your intuitiveness, insight, and wisdom."
Rena Tarbet, Independent National Sales Director, Dallas, TX

"In a manner that is authentic, graceful, and life-giving, Anne Johns has found a way to tap deeply into the goodness, wisdom, and strength of God. She writes from the heart, drawing us with her into the ingenuity and power of the living God. This is the real thing spiritually, and it is written with great skill and intelligence."
William J. Abraham, D. Phil
Southern Methodist University, Perkins School of Theology

"Anne Johns' gift for communicating her heart, especially through the daily prayers, is incredibly uplifting and refreshing. She is able to perfectly capture how I feel on a daily basis with words I couldn't find in my heart. *Java Time!* blends meaningful insights with a fresh, creative approach to challenge the working woman to aspire to be more like Jesus."
Jennifer Young
Christian Recording Artist

"Rather than using that 10-minute break complaining to co-workers, instead using *Java Time!* along with them is a way to become refreshed together in God's way for His purposes."
Elizabeth Ritz, Director
Prestonwood Pregnancy Center, Dallas, TX

"For years, I have searched for a daily devotional book geared toward the spiritual growth of a working woman. With time restrictions and growing responsibilities of being a working mother, this ten minute per day book provides a brief study of Scripture and true application to our lives as working women."
Mary E. Hamrick, Executive Director, Dragonfly Ministries

"Anne Johns writing is God-inspired, catchy, and to the point. From each brief overview of the daily scripture, I was intrigued to read more from the Bible and was challenged with the thought-provoking, relational type questions. I also felt the coffee recipes were an added bonus. I was uplifted using the book and felt good about myself when I finished the day."
Laura Beagles, The Academy of Christian Studies
Highland Park Methodist Church, Dallas, TX

"I loved *Java Time!* I was reading it for evaluation, but found myself involved in worship on each page. It's wonderful. Reading it took me to the throne."
Pam Chandler, Prestonwood Baptist Church Librarian, Dallas, TX

"Because God has called us to a ministry that emphasizes the Christian's personal relationship with Jesus Christ, we rejoice in the publication of *Java Time!* The fact that the author is our daughter-in-law is incidental! Anne shares our desire to help God's children find and maintain an abiding relationship with Him. Our prayer is that *Java Time!* will provide encouragement to the working woman in taking meaningful steps toward true fellowship with the Lover of our souls."
Jim and Kaye Johns, authors, Praying to Make a Difference

Java for women time!

Spiritual Refreshment
for Working Christian Women

ANNE JOHNS

Evergreen PRESS

TABLE OF CONTENTS

DEDICATION

Java Time! is dedicated to my wonderful family—Alvin and Lois Epstein, Michael and Stephen and their families, and to my children Ariana and Cyrus and their father Mehrdad Bavarian.

And especially, to David, my spiritual hero.

ACKNOWLEDGMENTS

The author wishes to acknowledge and thank the Lord for the inspiration, insight, direction, encouragement, and guidance of...
- David Johns, my husband and best friend, who suggested I speak to...
- Kelvin Foley, who met me for lunch and introduced me to...
- Brenda Josee, who helped me to attend CBA where I met...
- Keith Carroll and Brian Banashak, who took a serious interest in *Java Time!*

Thanks also to:
- Pastor Jack Graham, Prestonwood Baptist Church, who blessed this project
- Zig Ziglar, Pat Fortenberry, Dr. Billy Abraham, Jim and Kaye Johns, Christa Hoopes, Tamatha Davis, Dr. Elizabeth Ritz, Jamie McCrary, Jennifer Young, Mary Hamrick, Rena Tarbet, Karen Taylor, Pam Chandler, Anne Holland, Jack Dahlen, Kay Williams, Laurie Magers, and others who generously reviewed, edited, and endorsed *Java Time!*
- To Tim Scheer for his photographic genius.

And to my many Christian sisters and brothers who ran the race with me.

INTRODUCTION
Bean There, Done That!

Are you a working woman? Are you busy? Is your busy-ness leaving you overwhelmed, out of sorts and running on empty? If so, it's time to refuel. It's time for some serious spiritual refreshment, so gather up your favorite cup and bring along your Bible. It's *Java Time!*

Let's face it. Whether we're church volunteers or highly paid corporate executives, we are always on the job. By the time we roll out the door we've been up for hours, micro-managing every personal and family detail with the grace of an orchestra conductor on a full-throttle train ride.

It's tough out there. We forge ahead through traffic jams, trundle through parking lots, plunge into packed elevators and wait endlessly in the slowest moving line. Many of us arrive at offices that are littered with post-it notes, urgent e-mails, and rambling telephone messages. We're behind schedule even before we sit down.

It's even more challenging for the working Christian woman. Be honest, ladies, how much time do we really spend with the Lord before heading out in the morning?

Women of the real world—percolate! Quit singin' the coffee-house blues. Reach for your coffee mugs—and your Bible—and unite. It's Java Time with Jesus!

Java Time with Jesus

Ohhhh, how we love our coffee breaks! That 10-minute retreat from chaos and responsibility often helps us get through the work day. That frothy, steaming, creamy pick-me-up really hits the spot, doesn't it?

Now our coffee break can provide additional refreshment. In the time it takes to brew, pour and drink up, we can enter the Lord's presence and delight in His encouragement, loving direction, and spiritual guidance.

It's not by chance that you're here. You've been specially selected to meet the Boss over a cup of coffee. He's issued the invitation, so go for it. Whether you're enjoying a gourmet cappuccino in an up-scale coffeehouse, or a pot of office brew in the break room, come just as you are. You supply the coffee. Jesus Christ will supply the rest.

Not the Same Old Grind

This Bible study won't be a grind. In fact, it's designed to fill your cup, not empty it. Here's what *Java Time* is all about:

It's about building a relationship, not following a religion. God desires that we experience the abundant life right here, right now. The route to the Promised Land—a place of security, peace, confidence, joy and abundance—is through a relationship with Him. *Java Time* will help show you how!

It's about a process, not an event. Your foray into the Promised Land requires undergoing a significant process of change. The change includes asking for God's help, being willing to change and cultivating a desire to receive His best as we prove ourselves able. *Java Time* will help show you how!

It's about growing daily. God proved His faithfulness in the wilderness, but an entire generation of complaining, quarreling Israelites never reached the Promised Land. What kept them from receiving their inheritance? How can you avoid the same fate? *Java Time* will help show you how!

It's about expressing thankfulness. God longs to share His bounty. How do we express our thankfulness? *Java Time* will help show you how!

It's about becoming intentional. Building a relationship with

God takes time. Only by intentionally seeking Him will we be able to enter the Promised Land. That's where we'll find the insight, the reward, the intimacy and the wisdom that He longs to share. *Java Time!* will help show you how!

It's about expressing your needs and receiving an answer. Through Moses, God established an elaborate system to bring the Israelites into a right relationship with Him. Through Christ, we are able to express our concerns, petitions and praise directly before God without being hampered by ritual, sacrifice or ceremony. Through the Holy Spirit, we are able to receive spiritual guidance, direction, encouragement and correction. The way is open to anyone who seeks to understand. *Java Time* will help show you how!

It's about receiving the blessing. As the new generation of Israelites proved themselves to be able to care for what God was about to give them, He willingly gave them more and more. Though they conquered more land and won more battles, it was the powerful, personal relationship with Jehovah that became the greatest blessing of all. Is that what you want? *Java Time* will help show you how!

It's about working Christian women helping other women. The common experience of hundreds of working women—believers and non-believers alike—has resulted in a study that meets a majority of needs. The testimonies and blessings that come out of your experience will serve as an encouragement to others who may not know the Lord. Become a source of encouragement! *Java Time* will help show you how!

To the Bitter End

To explain how *Java Time!* evolved, let's go back a few years to a coffee break conversation that I had with Pat Fortenberry, a successful businesswoman. She asked me about my family, dreams, and goals. I told her how unhappy I was in my professional and personal life, and then I broke into tears.

She took a sip of coffee and then looked me square in the eye. "Anne, don't you realize that *everything that's ever happened to you—both the good and the bad—has brought you precisely to this very moment, to prepare you for what you are about to do?*"

That was exactly the knock-upside-the-head kind of lesson that God can use to bring a woman to her senses. A radical, exciting and supernatural relationship was about to unfold! But, was I ready?

Ready? Yes. Willing? No.

Here I was, a well-educated, task-focused woman who spent every day dashing, jumping, strafing and snaking my way through professional and personal challenges as if I were running a gauntlet. No wonder I was so tired, unhappy, disoriented, and alone. My conversation with Pat was the first in a chain of supernatural events that would eventually bring me to my knees. Broken and exhausted, I desperately wanted relief. My material idols, however, were no longer filling the void. I had had enough.

Emptying the Cup

Not long afterwards, I accepted Christ as Lord and Savior. I studied, read and tried to live the Christian life. But still, something was not right. There was no peace.

Then, one night I wrestled with sleep. Preoccupation and anxiety about the future kept me tossing and turning. Finally, I kicked back the covers and tip-toed into the kitchen. After brewing up some Arabica, I made my way into the living room, a small night light illuminating my path.

My beautiful indoor cactus garden threw a praise-filled silhouette onto the wall. The fish tank hummed and trickled quietly. I settled onto the sofa, cocooning myself in my grandmother's afghan, sipped long and slow and closed my eyes.

For the first time, I got real with God. I begged Him for help. Where was this abundant life I had been promised? Why were things still so hard? I was trying my best to be a "good" Christian woman—putting my family before my career, tithing faithfully, going to church, attending studies, and reading the Bible. Why did I feel so alone, scared and overwhelmed? Speak to me, God!

Tasting the Promise

It's amazing what you'll get when you ask. As I reached for the Bible on the coffee table, I absent-mindedly flipped through the worn pages. Then, I caught sight of Proverbs 8:17-21.

I love those who love me, and those who seek me find me. With me are riches and honor, enduring wealth and prosperity. My fruit is better than fine gold; what I yield surpasses choice silver. I walk in the way of righteousness, along the paths of justice, bestowing wealth on those who love me and making their treasuries full (NIV).

The promises seemed to jump off the page:

love • riches • honor • enduring wealth • prosperity
fine gold • choice silver • wealth • treasuries

Then, I heard a voice. Small, almost imperceptible, it lodged in my spirit. "Me," the voice said convictingly. "What about Me?"

I heard it again. It was the Holy Spirit reminding me how off track I was. I had become so task-focused, goal-oriented, and outcome-driven that I was missing the whole point of the scripture. The "stuff" had become more important than the Source of all the blessings.

The Holy Spirit had brought the truth to light. The Promised Land was not somewhere off in the distance and available only to a select few. It was offered freely, and I only had to reach out and receive it.

"My fruit is better than fine gold, what I yield surpasses choice silver."

"Where do I begin?" I asked Him. "I don't even *know* You!"

"Seek me."

"HOW?"

"Spend time with Me. Talk to Me. Listen to Me. Read the key Scripture again. But this time, read it carefully. The secret to what you are looking for is right here."

In other words…"Everything resonates and emanates from My hand. Your success is based on a give-and-take relationship between you and Me. When you seek Me, you will find what you are really looking for—the richness of peace, the honor of purpose, and wealth to share with others."

In that instant, the Holy Spirit had placed a plan of action into my hands. Suddenly, I knew where I needed to go. I had the tools to make it happen. I had a loving God waiting for me with outstretched arms. The rest was up to me.

The Perfect Brew for *Java Time!*

Do you sense a fragrant, refreshing opportunity beckoning to you? Can you devote your 10-minute coffee break to digging up the treasure that awaits you at the hand of the Source? Then, let's get started. Here's your recipe for success!

JAVA TIME!
Coffee or beverage of your choice
This book
A pen
A small Bible
A willing heart
A quiet place

Directions:
Blend your ingredients and pour yourself into *Java Time!* Allow to steep for 10-15 uninterrupted minutes!

Serving Suggestions:
Add a dash of peace! Allow God to infuse you with calm as you return to your workplace assignments. You'll find that you will think more creatively, exercise more patience, take God-honoring action, and be more effective in everything you do.

Stir in some sparkling blessings. Read Proverbs 8:17-21. That's what's in it for you.

Whip up some encouragement. This super brew is guaranteed to help you make a difference in the lives of others—both on the job and at home.

So, ladies, grab your mug.
See you in the break room!

Java Break: Effectiveness

WEEK 1 - DAY 1

Elaine's Story*

"As the child of two professional parents, I was brought up to think that being effective meant being productive. I was rewarded when I did well at school but punished if I fell short of someone else's expectations—usually my parents' and teachers'. As I grew into maturity, I took on the world's view of effectiveness. I became very good at setting goals, reaching them, and expecting material reward for doing so. I was consistently able to produce positive results—ones that were measured in dollars and cents.

"But as a working woman, things soon got out of hand. No matter how hard I applied myself, I never seemed to enjoy success. I was steeped in a kind of bitter brew that permeated everything and everyone around me. My personal and professional life suffered. I didn't like myself at all.

"One day, an e-mail circulated about a carrot, an egg, and coffee. In

* Note: the women pictured in this book are models and not the actual storytellers.

1

the story, a young woman asks her mom to explain why things had gotten so hard for her. Her mother boiled three pots of water and put a carrot in the first, an egg in the second, and some ground coffee beans in the third. In a few minutes, the carrots had gotten soft, the egg had gotten hard, but the coffee had released a wonderful aroma.

"Her mom explained that each had reacted differently to its environment. The carrot went into the boiling water strong and came out weak. The egg had gone in weak and came out strong. But the coffee released its wonderful aroma into the air and changed the water in which it was boiled.

"I considered the message in my own life. I understood that being effective in the workplace wasn't about deadlines or dollars, the lack of resources or having to work with others who may have different values. I understood that if I was to be effective—both on and off the job—I would have to become like a coffee bean."

Ask yourself...
To be effective, do you need to become
a carrot, an egg or a coffee bean?

On Being Effective

Being effective. The material world would like us to believe that it means being capable of producing a result—one often measured in dollars and cents. Is this what being effective means to you?

Given the pressures we women face on the job, it's no wonder that we feel ineffective from time to time. Have you ever heard yourself say:

- *These deadlines are impossible to meet!*
- *Without additional resources, there's no way I can do this project!*

- *No matter how hard I apply myself, I don't seem to have any success!*

God's guidelines for living and working effectively come from a relationship with Him—not from the world's arbitrary definition of accomplishment, success, or achievement. To the Lord, being effective means being organized, patient, and genuine. It means being the kind of woman who is able to allow Him to encourage, strengthen, build, direct, and walk with her as she makes her way through daily choices. Are you this kind of woman?

We all can benefit from a change of heart in the area of effectiveness. This changed "heart attitude" will become the focus of your time with the Lord over the next few days. At the end of the week, you may have a new perspective on what it means to be effective. And, most important, you may acquire valuable tools to help you realize your full, mature potential.

As you proceed through the week's exercises and undergo a process of formation into His likeness, pay attention to how the Lord partners with you. Ask yourself some questions:

- How is He reaching His desired goal in my life?
- How is He helping me become a real reflection of Him, His nature and ways?
- How have I shown my resemblance to Him in my interaction with others?

Watch your relationship with Him blossom as your interaction grows. Experience a new sense of freedom in the way you relate to Him and to others. By the end of the week, you'll emerge with a fresh new attitude—one that will bring you closer to the Promised Land. Hopefully, it will be one that you'll feel encouraged to share!

Enjoy your brew!

WEEK 1 - DAY 2

TODAY'S SELECTED BREW: 1 Samuel 18:14

> *In everything he did*
> *he had great success, because*
> *the Lord was with him.*

This passage concerns the relationship between an employer and his employee. King Saul, a proud and jealous superior, plotted against David—a young, respected, capable commander in his army. David recognized the danger he was in, but in order to remain effective, he continued to exhibit loyalty and humility. He did his job because he had been assigned an important responsibility. In order to be effective at what he did, he turned to God and asked for spiritual protection. God gave him what he asked for, and more. He had great success in all that he did because he knew who the real Boss was.

CUPPA INSPIRATION

1. David was effective in all that he did despite his on-the-job circumstances. The passage gives you the secret to his success. What was it?

_____

2. Have you ever felt ineffective at work? What might be the reason for this experience?

_____

3. David depended upon God around the clock. What does depending on God mean to you?

HEAVENLY AROMA

Lord God, I believe I am willing and ready to know You in a deeper, more real way. Father, I know it's not by chance that I come before Your throne today. Although You have been an ever-present reality in my life, now I long for a deeper understanding of You and Your ways. Thank you for paving the way from my door to Yours. Now I ask that You swing wide the portal and reveal Yourself to me in a powerful new way. Open my spiritual eyes to receive Light. Clear my ears to receive the Word. Cleanse me of the unworthiness I feel standing before the Creator of the Universe! As a step toward You, I bring one of many concerns—how to truly depend on You as I strive to be effective in all that I do. Help me understand Your will, Lord, as I struggle especially with:_____

_____.

REFRESHED AND RENEWED

Remember, more of God's blessings are given to those who properly take care of what they already have. What insights have you sensed God sharing with you today? How might you begin putting them into action?

_____

_____

_____

WEEK 1 - DAY 3

TODAY'S SELECTED BREW: Genesis 1:31

> *God saw all that he had made,*
> *and it was very good.*

The Book of Genesis is a book of beginnings. It recounts the majestic origin of the universe and the creation of man. In the exquisite detailing of the creation of the earth, God reveals His ultimate effectiveness: His plan, His organization, His follow-through. And most important, His crowning achievement—His creation of us!

CUPPA INSPIRATION

1. God used His skill to create a universe that would ultimately reflect His glory. Who does your work ultimately glorify? God? Your boss? Yourself?

_____

2. God's effectiveness is not based on haphazard guesswork or flimsy follow-through. Instead, He is effective because His efforts are focused on a magnificent outcome. Each and every action contributes to His divine purpose. Do you have a similar focus or passion for the work that you do?

_____

3. Look back through your life. Where have you been most effective? Of what do you think the Lord is most pleased?

_____

_____

HEAVENLY AROMA

Lord and the One who perfects, I come before you today with a heart filled with gratitude. How wonderful it is that You are available to me throughout the day! The door to Your heavenly throne room is always swung wide in anticipation of the moments we can have together. Thank You for being so gracious and loving with someone as impatient as I. Lord, how elegantly You have created everything. I am amazed at the complexity of the world around me. Down to the smallest detail, I can see Your magnificent hand at work. Even in my own life, Lord. You have given me a pliable and responsive heart, a mind that dances with purpose and direction, hands and feet to bear witness of Your love to all the world, a soul overflowing with creative potential, and a spirit that shines like a beacon, capable of illuminating the way for others. But, Father, I know I fall short of maturity. Let me not fall short of effectiveness because of my own lack of confidence. Let not the confusion and pride of the material world pull my gaze away from You. Build humility into my character, Lord, and remind me daily that my effectiveness lies in You, and not in:_____

_____ .

REFRESHED AND RENEWED

What insights have you sensed God sharing with you today? How might you begin putting them into action? God wants to see you respond to His loving guidance, correction, encouragement and counsel.

_____

_____

_____

WEEK 1 - DAY 4

TODAY'S SELECTED BREW: Deuteronomy 8:17-18

> *You may say to yourself, "My power and the strength of my hands have produced this wealth for me." But remember the Lord your God, for it is he who gives you the ability to produce wealth.*

The Israelites were on the verge of entering the Promised Land when Moses gives them his farewell address. In this emotional exhortation, he reviewed the covenant which bound them together as God's chosen people. He reminded them of God's provision throughout the lean and difficult desert years and warned them to guard against pride and self-righteousness as they entered into a life of comparative luxury in the Promised Land.

CUPPA INSPIRATION
1. Women are led to believe that on-the-job effectiveness and ultimate success are in their own hands. According to the scripture, is this true or false?

_____

2. The scripture says that the Lord gives us the ability to produce wealth. What does "wealth" mean to the world? To you?

_____

_____

_____

3. The scripture suggests that we should "remember the Lord" for His part in giving us the ability to produce wealth. How do you "remember the Lord"?

_____

_____

_____

HEAVENLY AROMA

Elohim, Manna of the Desert, today more than ever before, I acknowledge that all provision flows from Your unseen, faithful hands. In my own restless, achievement-oriented heart, I am humbled to realize how far I have allowed myself to be led away from You, the Source of all. You are the great Provider. I confess, with shame, that I have believed in a lie—that my success, effectiveness, and wealth depend only on myself. Have I created an idol in my reflection, Lord? Have my day-to-day concerns separated me from receiving Your best? If so, Father, break open my heart. Allow my self-centeredness to flow out, to empty the chamber and make a holy room for You above all else. Teach me Your ways, Lord, as I offer myself as a living sacrifice of time and talent. Accept my humble offering as a testimony to my commitment. Enable me to reflect Your effectiveness, and not my own, especially as I begin to: _____

_____ .

REFRESHED AND RENEWED

God wants to see you respond to His loving guidance, correction, encouragement and counsel. Remember, more of God's blessings are given to those who properly take care of what they already have. What insights have you sensed God sharing with you today? How might you begin putting them into action?

_____

_____

_____

9

Java Break: Effectiveness

WEEK 1 - DAY 5

TODAY'S SELECTED BREW: Mark 9:33-34

> *They came to Capernaum. When he was in the house, he asked them, "What were you arguing about on the road?" But they kept quiet because on the way they had argued about who was the greatest.*

This scripture comes from the Gospel of Mark, which records the events of Christ's public ministry, the training of the disciples, and the final events leading up to His crucifixion and resurrection. In this passage, the disciples were headed toward Peter's house, their campaign headquarters. Along the way, Christ explained His impending death to them, but being more preoccupied with themselves, they did not grasp the full impact of what He said. Instead, their conversation turned to who was the greatest among them. Worldly success, recognition, ambition, and pride had pushed them to greatly overvalue themselves. When Christ rebuked them, they were ashamed.

CUPPA INSPIRATION

1. Do you spend much time comparing yourself and your achievements to those of others at the workplace or in your industry? _____

2. Have you ever been in a situation where you and your co-workers talked about other people's competence behind their backs? _____

3. Being effective on the job requires teamwork and flexibility. Do you find yourself trying to take credit for work that others have performed?

_____

_____

HEAVENLY AROMA

Crowning Glory, You are the great Alpha and Omega, the beginning and end, the perfection to which I should aspire. How many times have I tried to steal Your glory? How humiliating it is to realize that I am caught up in the struggle for meaning and recognition, so that I can be better than the rest. Lord, I am just one woman trying to make a difference. Why do I feel overwhelmed sometimes? Protect me from my own overactive sense of self-importance. Let me not be a victim of pride, idolatry, or temptation. Make me a better team player. Provide opportunities for me to recognize the contributions of others and to keep from comparing myself to them. Be my stronghold against insecurity. Help me recognize that through You, I can be more effective, particularly in the area of: _____

_____ .

REFRESHED AND RENEWED

Remember, more of God's blessings are given to those who properly take care of what they already have. What insights have you sensed God sharing with you today? How might you begin putting them into action? God wants to see you respond to His loving guidance, correction, encouragement and counsel.

_____

_____

_____

Java Break: Effectiveness

WEEK 1 - DAY 6

COFFEE CAKE, SCONES AND DONUTS

Today, you have the opportunity to reflect over the insights God revealed during the week. In doing so, you'll bake up a treat to share with someone else! Please check the statements that reflect your relationship-building experience over the past few days:

☐ I'm learning more about expressing thankfulness.
☐ I'm expressing my needs in a way that builds my confidence in God.
☐ I'm receiving answers in a variety of ways.
☐ I'm experiencing new blessings.
☐ I'm involved in a process of change—making character adjustments as God inspires me.
☐ I see myself growing in my spiritual walk each day.
☐ I'm becoming intentional about building a relationship with God.

This week's *Java Time! with the Lord* focused on becoming an effective woman—both on and off the job. Please reflect, review, and restate the insights you've received along the way, as well as the heart attitude changes you have begun to incorporate into your life:

1. What inspirational insights are you seeing that will help you become more effective?

_____

_____

_____

2. What heart attitude changes are you making?

_____

_____

_____

3. As you continue to build your relationship with the Lord, where, how, or with whom can you share your insights on what it means to become more effective?

_____

_____

_____

ANGEL KISS COFFEE

To 1/3 cup ground coffee, add 1/2 tsp. nutmeg and 1/2 tsp. hazelnut, chocolate, or similar flavoring. Blend. Pour into a filter and brew as usual. Makes about 8 cups. Remember to share!

Java Break: Balance

WEEK 2 - DAY 1

Amy's Story

"I can't tell you how much pressure I experienced as a woman of the '80s. The entire thrust of my young adulthood was spent proving to everyone that I was the ideal Helen Reddy superwoman. "I am woman, hear me roar..." A balanced life back then meant striving to be independent, strong, and successful on my own terms. It had nothing to do with being content with being a woman, wife, mother, or friend. It had nothing to do with managing my time and maintaining my health and spiritual balance.

"When I graduated college and started working, I became more like a machine than a person. My work encroached on my personal time until there was no distinction between office and home. I socialized with my co-workers, became involved in activities that enhanced my career, and started putting in more and more time at the office. I wanted to prove myself worthy of the fast track I had designed for myself. I was miserable, tired, and had no life outside the office. I had no time for anything but making money.

"One afternoon I was trying to reconcile my checkbook but it just wouldn't balance. I became more and more aggravated until I realized that I was working myself sick over pennies. Some super woman, huh?

"At that moment I understood that my life had become a series of reconciliations rather than rewards. Instead of enjoying life, I was constantly apologizing to people for letting them down, missing important occasions, arriving late, leaving early, forgetting birthdays, that kind of thing—all for the sake of money. In my desire to become a superwoman, I had lost sight of what it meant to simply be a woman. My life was sadly out of balance. The pennies in my checkbook register had become more important than the accumulation of true riches. Needless to say, I was ready for a change."

Ask yourself...
Are you better at counting pennies
or accumulating true riches?

On Living a Balanced Life

Balance. With the many responsibilities women have, it's easy to become overwhelmed and out of sorts. Family, social, work, personal and spiritual needs often compete, leaving us feeling guilty, saddened, or bitter.

Does living a balanced life mean you have to be all things to all people? Have you heard yourself say:

- *I'm always taking care of everyone else's needs. What about my own?"*
- *If only I had more time, I'd (go back to school, lose weight, learn to paint, relax more...)*
- *If I spend more time on my career now, I'll be able to retire a lot sooner!"*

What does God say about living a balanced life? Ecclesiastes 3:1-8 says:

There is a time for everything, and a season for every activity under heaven: a time to be born and a time to die, a time to plant and a time to uproot, a time to kill and a time to heal, a time to tear down and a time to build, a time to weep and a time to laugh, a time to mourn and a time to dance, a time to scatter stones and a time to gather them, a time to embrace and a time to refrain, a time to search and a time to give up, a time to keep and a time to throw away, a time to tear and a time to mend, a time to be silent and a time to speak, a time to love and a time to hate, a time for war and a time for peace.

Who has God given us as a model of pure balance? The perfect, fully human being of Christ. Though His job was to reveal the Father to humanity and display the image and likeness of God, He still took time to celebrate, to rest, to pray, to teach, to minister, and to be a friend.

The world puts much more emphasis on the physical and material than on the spiritual. Living a balanced life means eliminating distractions, simplifying processes, and not dwelling in the extremes—removing anything that is contrary to God-honoring work and life experience. It means simplifying our routines, reevaluating our expectations, setting up boundaries, acting with forethought, being a peacemaker, and thinking through decisions.

We all can benefit from a change of heart in the area of effectiveness. This changed "heart attitude" will become the focus of your time with the Lord over the next few days. At the end of the week, you may have a new perspective on what it means to be effective. And, most important, you may acquire valuable tools to help you realize your full potential.

As you proceed through the week's exercises, pay attention to how the Lord begins to partner with you. Watch your relationship with Him blossom as your interaction grows. Experience a new sense of freedom in the way you relate to others. By the end of the week, you'll emerge with a fresh new attitude—one that will bring you closer to all the blessings He wants to bestow upon you. Hopefully, it will be one that you'll feel encouraged to share!

Fill your cup to the brim!

WEEK 2 - DAY 2

TODAY'S SELECTED BREW: Romans 12:2

> *Do not conform any longer to the pattern of this world, but be transformed by the renewing of your mind. Then you will be able to test and approve what God's will is— His good, pleasing and perfect will.*

Paul's letter to the Romans was written on his third missionary journey. He was preparing to leave for Palestine with the collection he had gathered for the poor saints in Jerusalem. This letter offers instruction to the new believers on topics related to living a balanced life.

CUPPA INSPIRATION

1. In this passage, Paul instructs the believers not to "conform" to the material world. What does this mean to you?

_____

_____

2. The passage suggests that we should be "transformed by the renewing of our mind." In a world where our mind is constantly tempted by the material, the sensual, and the emotional, what does it mean to "renew" the mind?

_____

_____

_____

3. God wants you to experience balance in your life. If you are exhausted, unhappy, or tired at work (according to the scripture), what might this mean?

_____

_____

_____

HEAVENLY AROMA

Lord, Spring of Living Water, there are areas in my life that are out of balance. I know this is true because of the stress and preoccupation I experience. When I should be thankful, I am worried. When I should be calm, I am irritated. When I should be quiet, I am agitated. Where does this come from, Lord? Have I become so conformed to this world that I have lost the youthful sense of simplicity, peace, calm, and joy that You intend for me? Help me renew my mind, Lord. Help me sense Your Holy presence beckoning me toward simplicity, faith, and rest. This is the path that glorifies You. Teach me to say "no" and to eliminate everything that does not enhance my walk with You. Help me rest, Lord. Let me begin by honoring Your Sabbath and keeping it holy, remaining for a while in that quiet, sanctified place where I can begin to know You better. Help me live a more balanced life, particularly in the area of: _____

_____ .

REFRESHED AND RENEWED

What insights have you sensed God sharing with you today? How might you begin putting them into action? God wants to see you respond to His loving guidance, correction, encouragement and counsel! Remember, more of God's abundance is given to those who properly take care of what they've already been given.

_____

_____

_____

WEEK 2 - DAY 3

TODAY'S SELECTED BREW: 2 Corinthians 6:14

Do not be yoked together with unbelievers.
For what do righteousness and wickedness
have in common? Or what fellowship can
light have with darkness?

This is the second letter that the Apostle Paul wrote to the believers at Corinth. The passage addresses the balance we should seek to maintain in our relationships with others. It implies that we should avoid relationships with those who may force us to compromise our values and belief systems. This warning extends to those entertainments and business transactions that women in the work world face every day.

CUPPA INSPIRATION

1. As a working woman, do you find that the work world tempts you to participate in certain amusements and business transactions that are not in keeping with your Christian faith? How?

_____

_____

2. Do you spend more time with non-believing friends or true believers? Do you perceive a difference in character between the two?

_____

_____

3. Do you make time for church? Prayer? Bible study? Ministry? Why or why not?

_____

_____

_____

HEAVENLY AROMA

Compassionate and gracious God, the truth that you reveal today is profound and hard to assimilate, but it is truth nevertheless. I understand that there is no harmony, peace, or balance in my life when I surround myself with busy-ness, with people and activities that are not compatible with Your goals for my life, with activities that do not bring me into Your perfect peace, and with relationships that do not honor You. Sometimes I feel that I am spinning out of control. So often, I yield to the interests of money, prestige, and recognition, especially at work. Then, exhausted, I fall into a pattern of deception, thinking that if I work harder, or yield to the pressures or temptations of the workplace, that it will all work itself out in the end. This viewpoint is out of balance with Your ways. Help me, Lord! Show me how to balance my life, particularly in the area of: _____

_____ .

REFRESHED AND RENEWED

God wants to see you respond to His loving guidance, correction, encouragement and counsel! Remember, more of God's abundance is given to those who properly take care of what they've already been given. What insights have you sensed God sharing with you today? How might you begin putting them into action?

_____

_____

_____

WEEK 2 - DAY 4

TODAY'S SELECTED BREW: Matthew 4:8-10

> *Again, the devil took Him to a very high mountain and showed Him all the kingdoms of the world and their splendor. "All this I will give you," he said, "if you will bow down and worship me." Jesus said to him, "Away from me, Satan! For it is written: 'Worship the Lord your God, and serve Him only.'"*

Matthew, a tax gatherer under the Romans, wrote the first of the four gospels—God's joyful messages to us—around A.D. 63. In this passage, he refers to Christ's 40 days in the wilderness in which He was tempted three times by Satan. Rather than responding by using psychology, manipulation or intellect, Christ used a powerful, personal weapon to ward off the enemy. He quoted scripture and caused the devil to retreat.

CUPPA INSPIRATION

1. The enemy is real. He is not a figment of the imagination. This enemy often appears as an "angel of light" who can easily tempt us into thinking that he represents the holiness of the Lord. However, this enemy angel exists to tempt and torture. What evidence is there in your life that shows the enemy is real?

_____

_____

_____

2. For everything that is physical and visible in our material world, there is a spiritual and invisible dynamic operating behind it. Why is it impossible to fight off spiritual attack using psychological, pharmaceutical and physical weapons?

_____

_____

3. What questions might you address to a depressed co-worker who comes to you for advice?

_____

_____

_____

HEAVENLY AROMA

Lord, Rock in whom I take refuge, I never really understood the role of the enemy in my life until now. Thank you for the wisdom of the scriptures, and the model of Christ as He faced His temptation. I now see that the enemy has taken me to high places where idolatry is practiced in my own life. He has tempted me to become self-reliant and materialistic. He has set me on a path toward stress, jealousy, and anger, and away from all that is right and holy and clean. Oh, Lord, thank you for Your Word—the only weapon I need against the wiles of the enemy. Thank you for Christ, the true Healer against fear, depression, addiction, and dependency. I ask You to woo me back to the simple comfort and quiet embrace of Your strong, protecting arms. Teach me to balance these, my needs:

_____ .

REFRESHED AND RENEWED

Remember, more of God's abundance is given to those who properly take care of what they've already been given. God wants to see you respond to His loving guidance, correction, encouragement, and counsel! What insights have you sensed God sharing with you today? How might you begin putting them into action?

_____

_____

_____

Java Break: Balance

WEEK 2 - DAY 5

TODAY'S SELECTED BREW: John 2:1-4

> *On the third day a wedding took place at Cana in Galilee. Jesus' mother was there, and Jesus and His disciples had also been invited to the wedding. When the wine was gone, Jesus' mother said to Him, "They have no more wine." "Dear woman, why do you involve me?" Jesus replied. "My time has not yet come."*

The book of John was given by inspiration to the brother of the Apostle James. Unlike the other disciples who were martyred, John died a natural death on the island of Patmos after writing the Book of Revelation. In this chapter, John gives us an account of Jesus' first miracle—turning water into wine while He was a guest at the marriage of a friend in Cana of Galilee.

CUPPA INSPIRATION

1. Jesus was a busy man. Nevertheless, he took time to attend a friend's wedding. Do you take time to cultivate relationships with believers outside of work?

2. A balanced life includes making time for God, family, work, friends, and self. What percentage of time do you spend on each? Is your schedule balanced?

3. List the activities you are currently involved in outside of work. Include sports, volunteer, community-related, hobbies, etc. If you could only choose one, which would it be? How does this honor God?

_____

_____

_____

HEAVENLY AROMA

Father, You are my sure foundation. I come to you exhausted from the rigors of life. I lay before You the burden of my daily responsibilities and the overflowing requirements of living in this material world. I desire release from the burden of carrying such weight alone. I have believed in a lie, Lord. I have listened to others who have placed a burden of blame on my shoulders for not being available to meet their needs around the clock. Teach me to balance my interests with those of others. Enable me to make enough time for both the physical and spiritual side of life. Help me create boundaries around the precious time I have to spend with You, with my family, and with those You have brought into my life. Create in me a repose, a sense of calm, and a willingness to rest, when faced with: _____

_____ .

REFRESHED AND RENEWED

What insights have you sensed God sharing with you today? How might you begin putting them into action? God wants to see you respond to His loving guidance, correction, encouragement and counsel! Remember, more of God's abundance is given to those who properly take care of what they've already been given.

_____

_____

_____

WEEK 2 - DAY 6

COFFEE CAKE, SCONES AND DONUTS

Today, you have the opportunity to reflect over the insights God revealed during the week. In doing so, you'll bake up a treat to share with someone else! Please check the statements that reflect your relationship-building experience over the past few days:

☐ I'm learning more about expressing thankfulness.

☐ I'm expressing my needs in a way that builds my confidence in God.

☐ I'm receiving answers in a variety of ways.

☐ I'm experiencing new blessings.

☐ I'm involved in a process of change—making character adjustments as God inspires me.

☐ I see myself growing in my spiritual walk each day.

☐ I'm becoming intentional about building a relationship with God.

This week's *Java Time with the Lord* focused on suggestions to create balance in your life—both on and off the job. Please reflect, review, and restate the insights you've received along the way, as well as the heart attitude changes you have begun to incorporate into your life:

1. What inspirational insights are you seeing that will help you develop more balance in your life.

_____

_____

_____

2. What heart attitude changes are you making?

_____

_____

_____

3. As you continue to build your relationship with the Lord, where, how or with whom can you share your insights on what it means to develop more balance in your life?

_____

_____

_____

Brew for the Bunch

Start with 8 cups of coffee, cooled to room temp. Put half in a pitcher and add a 14 oz. can of sweetened condensed milk, 1/2 cup of chocolate syrup, two cups half-and-half (ok, use skim milk if you must) and 4 cups of ice cubes. Stir well, then add the other four cups of coffee. Stir and serve up!

Java Break: Character

WEEK 3 - DAY 1

Marie's Story

"I have a lot of allergies, especially when it comes to certain fragrances. Sometimes they make me nauseous, and other times my eyes water or I get a headache. Obviously, I can't tell my coworkers to quit wearing their perfume, so instead, I suffer in silence and stay by myself as much as possible.

"At Christmas, we had an office party and everyone had to exchange a small gift with a "secret" partner. I received some scented hand cream from my supervisor. I didn't want to offend her, so I said a quick prayer and spread some on my hands. Less than a minute later I was in the restroom clawing at the rash, trying to wash it off. My eyes teared, my sinuses closed up, and I got so nauseous I had to be sent home for the day.

"The other day, I was assigned a last-minute project with a woman whose work ethic is vastly different from my own. Not only is she undependable and manipulative, but she also wears an awful cologne.

"I knew it would be a struggle to meet the deadline working with her. Every day became a difficult challenge. I could just feel my blood pressure go up when she would show up late with an excuse for not having done the assignment for the day. Her character was negatively influencing my own attitude toward the job, and eventually, I was forced to confront her in the supervisor's office. Needless to say, she wasn't very enthusiastic about working with me from then on.

"In any case, I made an interesting observation about how a person's character is like the fragrance they wear. Had she been dependable, honest, trustworthy, fair—even friendly—I could have made an effort to work with her. But because her character was so flawed, it was a struggle even to try.

Character is the soul's fragrance. It impacts on everyone around you, leaving an unmistakable, lasting impression.

Ask yourself…
Does your "character perfume" attract people?
Or does it send them home feeling ill?

On Building Character

Character. In medieval times, convicted prisoners were branded with a "character" by the authorities—an individual letter symbolizing a crime such as "M" for murderer. One glance at the person's forehead or shoulder told a stranger what offense had been committed and what the guilty party's character was like. The brand stood for their lack of moral quality.

Today, we reveal our character in many ways. Through our words and actions, people around us can see what we're made of. Our character is judged based on the way we respond to, care for and encourage others, as well as the way that we follow through on the commitments we have made. When we listen quietly to the concerns of a friend, or offer a shoulder to lean on, our character is revealed. It's revealed when we rebound from a failure and try again and again. Whether good or bad, we can't hide our character—it's evident to everyone through our behavior.

It is said that life is like a grindstone. Whether you get *ground down* or *polished up* depends on you. Your character has nothing to do with your education. Rather, it's that part of you that shines forth when nobody's watching. Like the tree that falls in the forest—it still makes a sound, regardless of whether anyone is listening.

Though our character may appear invisible to us, it's quite obvious to others. Take Christ as an example. He was fully human, but observers couldn't help but notice that He was different. What did they recognize beneath His humanity that made Him so?

In the workplace, character development takes on a different meaning. It describes the process we go through when confronting difficult people or situations. It refers to the way we accept what we cannot change and the way we run our business. It means keeping our eyes focused on the interests of the employer and not on our own needs. It means meeting budgets, deadlines, and expectations with a positive attitude.

How is character developed? Through challenges and testing, and perhaps suffering. Character is developed by overcoming temptation and by speaking the truth in a loving way.

We all can benefit from a change of heart in the area of character. This changed "heart attitude" will become the focus of your time with the Lord over the next few days. At week's end, you may have a new perspective on what it means to have a God-honoring character. And, most important, you may acquire valuable tools to help you realize your full, mature potential.

Watch your relationship with the Lord blossom as your interaction grows this week. Experience a new sense of freedom in the way you relate to Him and to others as you develop your character—one day at a time.

Java Break: Character

WEEK 3 - DAY 2

TODAY'S SELECTED BREW: Romans 5:3-5

> *Not only so, but we also rejoice in our suffering, because we know that suffering produces perseverance; perseverance, character; and character, hope. And hope does not disappoint us, because God has poured out His love into our hearts by the Holy Spirit, whom he has given us.*

Romans 5 addresses what every person fears the most—suffering. However, in this letter to the Romans, Paul demonstrates the blessing that comes from our day-to-day trials and pressures and is the very essence of what builds character.

CUPPA INSPIRATION

1. According to this scripture, difficult circumstances are designed to yield three outcomes. What are they?

_____

_____

2. Paul says that hope springs from character. Why is hope important for the working woman to have, in light of work challenges such as stress, downsizing, and layoffs?

_____

_____

_____

3. What challenges are you facing in your day-to-day work environment that are contributing to the development of your character?

_____

_____

_____

HEAVENLY AROMA

Lord, my Shield, I never thought I would thank you for the difficulties I am facing today. It never occurred to me that You are calling me to a greater blessing. I understand now that each challenge I face has been ordained by You for the greater purpose of building and polishing my character. I try to avoid pain and suffering, and I tend to take the easy way out in order to steer clear of confrontation and conflict. But there they are—the consequences of my own choices in life—teaching me lessons, one after the other. Lord, help me find meaning in each character-building challenge. Free me from my fears about pain and suffering, and produce in me a sense of optimism in the face of conflict. Help me draw a line in the sand, across which the enemy can no longer trespass. Let this be my place of refuge in You, as you continue to build my perseverance, character and hope. Renew my confidence in You, Lord, especially in the area of: _____

_____ .

REFRESHED AND RENEWED

God wants to see you respond to His loving guidance, correction, encouragement and counsel! Remember, more of God's abundance is given to those who properly take care of what they've already been given. What insights have you sensed God sharing with you today? How might you begin putting them into action?

_____

_____

_____

WEEK 3 - DAY 3

TODAY'S SELECTED BREW: Matthew 5:43-45

> *You have heard that it was said, "Love your neighbor and hate your enemy," But I tell you: Love your enemies and pray for those who persecute you, that you may be sons of your Father in heaven. He causes His sun to rise on the evil and the good, and sends rain on the righteous and the unrighteous.*

Matthew 5 is the famous Sermon on the Mount—the longest and fullest continued discourse on record in all the Gospels. Here, Jesus addresses His followers about what they should do during their day and throughout their life. This passage focuses on the law of brotherly love.

CUPPA INSPIRATION

1. Do you work with people who may have different character values than your own?_____

_____

2. For whatever reason, God blesses both the good and the bad. Give two examples from the scripture that prove this is so.

_____

_____

_____

3. Many working women complain that they have been the target of

gossip, rumor-mongering and cliquish behavior at the workplace. What does the scripture suggest the Christian do in this case?

_____

_____

_____

HEAVENLY AROMA

Father who blesses the just and the unjust, there are so many things You despise: haughty eyes and lies, hands that shed innocent blood, hearts that scheme, feet that rush into evil, and lips that stir up dissension. Hear my confession. When I try to do good, evil is right there alongside me. Why is this, Lord? You have told me to love my neighbor as myself and to pray for those who persecute me. But sometimes it is hard. The real world is full of challenges— people with whom I cannot seem to get along. People who judge me rather than examine their own faults. And yet, I do the same. Polish my character and prepare me for all the blessings You have set aside in my name. Lord, help me forgive and pray for these that have harmed me, particularly this one: _____

_____ .

REFRESHED AND RENEWED

Remember, more of God's abundance is given to those who properly take care of what they've already been given. God wants to see you respond to His loving guidance, correction, encouragement and counsel! What insights have you sensed God sharing with you today? How might you begin putting them into action?

_____

_____

_____

WEEK 3 - DAY 4

TODAY'S SELECTED BREW—2 Chronicles 32:30-31

> *It was Hezekiah who blocked the upper outlet of the Gihon spring and channeled the water down to the west side of the City of David. He succeeded in everything he undertook. But when envoys were sent by the rulers of Babylon to ask Him about the miraculous sign that had occurred in the land, God left Him to test Him and to know everything that was in His heart.*

Hezekiah was a proud and arrogant king, best known for engineering a 1,700-foot passageway through solid rock to bring a permanent water supply to the people of Jerusalem. But when he fell sick and was miraculously healed, he failed to acknowledge God's hand in it. Despite his accomplishments, the Lord turned against Hezekiah and taught him a lesson. He took everything away from Hezekiah and his family because of his character flaw.

CUPPA INSPIRATION
1. According to the passage, what character flaw did Hezekiah exhibit?

_____

2. Pride, self-confidence, jealousy and a competitive nature seem to rule the workplace these days, just as they did in Hezekiah's time.

Why did God leave Hezekiah? What was He testing?

_____

_____

3. Do you ever feel as if God has tested your heart, or even "left" you? Based on Hezekiah's experience, why might that be?

_____

_____

_____

HEAVENLY AROMA

Lord, of all the earth, I realize that I have been proud and self-reliant most of my life. I confess before You that I am often arrogant, celebrating my own abilities rather than giving You the recognition You deserve. There have been times that I have neither stood for justice nor walked with integrity...times when I have conceived trouble and rushed into sin, turning my back on the One who loves me most...times I have been swift to judge others and even You. Soften my character, Lord. Search my heart and examine my mind. As water reflects a face, let my heart reflect the quality of a growing Christ-likeness. Build in me a character full of humility, dignity, strength, wisdom, and endurance in the face of today's challenge of:

_____

_____ .

REFRESHED AND RENEWED

What insights have you sensed God sharing with you today? How might you begin putting them into action? God wants to see you respond to His loving guidance, correction, encouragement and counsel! Remember, more of God's abundance is given to those who properly take care of what they've already been given.

_____

_____

_____

WEEK 3 - DAY 5

TODAY'S SELECTED BREW: Luke 16:10-12

> *Whoever can be trusted with very little can also be trusted with much, and whoever is dishonest with very little will also be dishonest with much. So if you have not been trustworthy in handling worldly wealth, who will trust you with true riches? And if you have not been trustworthy with someone else's property, who will give you property of your own?*

Luke was a Gentile physician and Paul's companion. He provides a summary of Christ's character, purpose, redemptive power, and will. In this passage, Luke presents a parable on how to manage what we've been given.

CUPPA INSPIRATION
1. Do you consider yourself a trustworthy person? How and why?

_____

_____

_____

2. Would you describe yourself as being "blessed" materially, emotionally, spiritually or financially? If not, can you explain why, in terms of this scripture?

_____

_____

_____

3. How might you begin proving to God that you have a character worthy of handling true riches?

_____

_____

_____

HEAVENLY AROMA

Lord, my Provider, today I want to begin building Your confidence in me. I begin by placing the flaws of my character before You, asking You to forgive the times when I was untrustworthy and dishonest with You. In my heart, I know that I have misused what You have so generously given to me. I have not always cared for those You have placed in my trust. I have invested my time, talent, and money in foolish endeavors. Sometimes I have even been dishonest. Lord, I lay before you the broken trust, the misguided decisions, and the character flaws in my life. I ask you to envelop me with your mercy and teach me a better way. Let me try again, Father, to be a conduit of trustworthiness. Help me become a woman who can be entrusted with much. For every blessing and resource You lay in my hand, may I be worthy to have, to hold and to use it all for Your glory. Let me begin today, Father, by:

_____ .

REFRESHED AND RENEWED

God wants to see you respond to His loving guidance, correction, encouragement and counsel! Remember, more of God's abundance is given to those who properly take care of what they've already been given. What insights have you sensed God sharing with you today? How might you begin putting them into action?

_____

_____

_____

Java Break: Character

WEEK 3 - DAY 6

COFFEE CAKE, SCONES AND DONUTS

Today, you have the opportunity to reflect over the insights God revealed during the week. In doing so, you'll bake up a treat to share with someone else! Please check the statements that reflect your relationship-building experience over the past few days:

☐ I'm learning more about expressing thankfulness.
☐ I'm expressing my needs in a way that builds my confidence in God.
☐ I'm receiving answers in a variety of ways.
☐ I'm experiencing new blessings.
☐ I'm involved in a process of change—making character adjustments as God inspires me.
☐ I see myself growing in my spiritual walk each day.
☐ I'm becoming intentional about building a relationship with God.

This week's *Java Time! with the Lord* focused on suggestions to build a more Christ-like character—both on and off the job. Please reflect, review and restate the insights you've received along the way, as well as the heart attitude changes you have begun to incorporate into your life:

1. What inspirational insights are you seeing that will help you develop a more Christ-like character?

_____
_____
_____

2. What heart attitude changes are you making?

_____

_____

_____

3. As you continue to build your relationship with the Lord, where, how or with whom can you share your insights on what it means to develop a more Christ-like character?

_____

_____

_____

**Workin'
Woman's Whistle Wetter**

Blend a half cup of cold coffee, half cup of pineapple juice and one cup of sherbet in a blender. Serve in shallow chilled glasses.
Close your eyes
and enjoy!

Java Break: Attitude

WEEK 4 - DAY 1

Ramona's story

"My supervisor comes from another country. As you can imagine, there are quite a few underlying cultural differences that impact the way we work together. Her attitude about everything is stern, cold, critical, and antagonistic. Mine is to be helpful, available, and responsive to the needs of my co-workers, especially since we work as a close-knit team with heavy deadlines and accountability.

"As time passed in our relationship, this supervisor became more and more difficult to work with. Every time I tried to help my co-workers, she would step in and tell me to mind my own business and go back to work. I'm a helper by nature, and I'm pretty good about meeting deadlines, so you can imagine how I felt when she came down on me for doing what I thought was right.

"One day, she called me into her office for my mid-year review. I was astonished at how dark the office was. She had not opened the blinds, so the little plants on her bookshelf were almost dead from thirst and lack of light.

"Suddenly a scripture came to me.

> *Are there not twelve hours of daylight? A man who walks by day will not stumble, for he sees by this world's light. It is when he walks by night that he stumbles, for he has no light* (John 11:9-10).

"I finally realized that this poor woman had no light in her life. No wonder she was miserable.

"Well, the mid-year review was not glowing. But I took it in stride. My real boss is Christ—not this unhappy supervisor.

"The next day I returned the mid-year review to her office while she was on her lunch break. I noticed she had thrown away the little plants that were so starved for light and water, so I took them out of the trash basket and brought them into my office. I lovingly watered them, talked to them, and sat them on my windowsill in the sunshine. As I tended the plants, I'd pray for her, asking Christ to soften her heart.

"Imagine her surprise when I brought the plants back to her, revived and blooming! She couldn't believe that I had been kind enough to do that for her, especially since she had been so negative towards me. Since that day, she has been much kinder to everyone on the job. By exemplifying Christian love, I believe I helped her to understand my true motivation. I stayed true to what I knew was right, prayed for her, and then rested in the confident knowledge that Christ would take care of the rest."

Ask yourself...
Whose plant needs watering at the workplace?

On Having the Right Attitude

Attitude. It's the one human freedom that cannot be taken away—

the choice of one's attitude in any given set of circumstances. Our choice of attitude is more important than any success or failure, any financial gain or any circumstance in which we find ourselves enmeshed. It either fuels us or cripples us.

How do your circumstances impact your attitude? How do negative attitudes affect your relationship with others? With God? What are the benefits of a positive attitude? Whose attitude should you imitate? These are the questions you'll explore with the Lord this week.

There are many opportunities in the workplace to reflect a God-honoring attitude. One way is by being thankful for the resources you have, rather than upset about the ones that are absent. Another way is to show yourself willing to work on projects that may not be as highly visible as others, but that still need to be done. A third way is to make a consistent effort to be cheerful, helpful, and available—even when others choose to do otherwise.

We all can benefit from a change of heart in the area of attitude. This changed "heart attitude" will become the focus of your time with the Lord over the next few days. At the end of the week, you will have a new perspective on what it means to have a Christ-like attitude. And, most important, you will acquire valuable tools to help you realize your full, mature potential.

As you proceed through the week's exercises and undergo a process of formation into His likeness, pay attention to how the Lord partners with you. Ask yourself some questions:

- How is He reaching His desired goal in my life?
- How is He helping me become a real reflection of Him, His nature and ways?
- How have I shown my resemblance to Him in my interaction with others?

Watch your relationship with Him blossom as your interaction grows. Experience a new sense of freedom in the way you relate to Him and to others. By the end of the week, you'll emerge with a fresh new attitude—one that will bring you closer to God's abundance for you. Hopefully, it will be one that you'll feel encouraged to share!

Enjoy your brew!

Java Break: Attitude

WEEK 4 - DAY 2

TODAY'S SELECTED BREW: Genesis 4:6-7

> *Then the Lord said to Cain, "Why are you angry? Why is your face downcast? If you do what is right, will you not be accepted? But if you do not do what is right, sin is crouching at your door; it desires to have you, but you must master it."*

Cain and Abel were sons of Adam and Eve. According to the custom of the time, both presented their "first fruits" to the Lord. However, Cain's gift of grain—a gift of his own labor—was probably offered up with a mechanical, non-devotional attitude, and therefore was unacceptable to God. His brother Abel offered a more acceptable sacrifice—one that required the shedding of an animal's blood. God suggested that Cain change his attitude, but Cain took out his rage and jealousy on his brother rather than follow God's advice.

CUPPA INSPIRATION

1. Cain's "downcast face" was physical evidence of his bad attitude. This must have affected those who observed him. Try checking your face periodically in the mirror throughout the day. Does your countenance reflect a positive or negative attitude? Why?

_____

_____

_____

2. Cain could have spent some time in prayer or self-examination when he understood that God had rejected his offering. Instead, he took the rejection and failure out on someone close to him. Have you ever been rejected? Did you spend time in prayer or self-examination or did you become angry or vindictive?

_____

_____

3. The scripture says that "if you do not do what is right, sin is crouching at your door; it desires to have you, but you must master it." How can a change in attitude empower you to "master sin"?

_____

_____

HEAVENLY AROMA
Lord, Firstborn over all creation, how many times I have let You down! How many times I have walked around with a downcast face and bad attitude when things didn't go my way. How often have I allowed sin to remain at my door when I could have discharged it with a heartfelt and urgent prayer. Lord, teach me how to do right in every situation, how to bring my best before You, how to work diligently and honor You in the process. Encourage me to bring my concerns before You instead of taking them out on those around me, especially today, as I face: _____

_____ .

REFRESHED AND RENEWED
Remember, more of God's abundance is given to those who properly take care of what they've already been given. God wants to see you respond to His loving guidance, correction, encouragement, and counsel! What insights have you sensed God sharing with you today? How might you begin putting them into action?

_____

_____

_____

Java Break: Attitude

WEEK 4 - DAY 3

TODAY'S SELECTED BREW: Exodus 14:15-16

> *Then the Lord said to Moses, "Why are you crying out to me? Tell the Israelites to move on. Raise your staff and stretch out your hand over the sea to divide the water so that the Israelites can go through the sea on dry ground."*

Exodus 14 has all the makings of a major motion picture with troops overtaking the terrified Israelites, a pillar of cloud leading the way, an anxious leader with despondent followers, the desert on one side and a raging Red Sea on the other. Given the circumstances, you can just imagine Moses' attitude in the face of a major life challenge!

CUPPA INSPIRATION

1. The scripture implies that Moses "cried out" to God when faced with an impossible situation. What does "crying out" mean to the faithful Christian?

_____

_____

2. God gave Moses specific instructions to raise his staff and stretch his hand over the sea. Figuratively speaking, what was Moses "stretching" when he obeyed God?

_____

_____

3. What challenge are you facing on the job that may require you to adjust your attitude in order to perform God-honoring work?

_____

_____

_____

HEAVENLY AROMA

Protector of my life, thank You for providing me a safe place to turn during my times of trouble. Thank You for taking on my concerns, my challenges, my fears. I confess that I need to cry out to You more often than I do. Why, Lord, do I tend to keep my burdens inside? Why do I often seek solutions on my own? Why do I seem to push You away in my anger, resentment, or fear? I know this is wrong. I ask You to forgive me and change my attitude about my circumstances and the events in life that I cannot control. Give me courage to test the waters—to stretch my faith muscle—to claim Your promises of protection and peace. Help me to cease striving in my own strength. Show Yourself as my ultimate refuge, a very present help in times of trouble. A resting place to unburden all that seeks to destroy me. Lead me, then, as the Good Shepherd You are, particularly as I face: _____

_____ .

REFRESHED AND RENEWED

What insights have you sensed God sharing with you today? How might you begin putting them into action? God wants to see you respond to His loving guidance, correction, encouragement and counsel! Remember, more of God's abundance is given to those who properly take care of what they've already been given.

_____

_____

_____

Java Break: Attitude

WEEK 4 - DAY 4

TODAY'S SELECTED BREW: Ruth 2:7

> *She said, "Please let me glean and gather among the sheaves behind the harvesters." She went into the field and has worked steadily from morning till now, except for a short rest in the shelter.*

The Book of Ruth is thought to have been written by Samuel. It recounts the story of a widowed young woman—a foreigner and a pagan—who returns to Israel with her mother-in-law Naomi rather than return to her own land. In Chapter 2, Ruth goes out to glean "leftover grain" in the field of Boaz (her kinsman redeemer) as was the custom of the day for the poor.

CUPPA INSPIRATION

1. Ruth's task was menial and degrading. But her consistent attitude toward the work showed that she was thankful. What is your attitude toward your work?

_____

_____

2. Boaz (a symbol of Christ to come) eventually married Ruth (symbolic bride of Christ—the Church). He saw something in her that appealed to him—beyond her physical beauty. Based on the scripture, what do you think attracted Boaz' attention?

_____

_____

3. Though Ruth experienced hard times, she remained confident that God, in His timing, would take care of the situation. Is it possible that God wants to test your attitude—as well as your character—to prepare you for a new opportunity? Or that He's watching how you respond to the challenges in your path now?

_____

_____

_____

HEAVENLY AROMA

Prince of Peace, thank You for the challenges of life that You have placed in my path. I believe that You are preparing me for a wonderful blessing, though I admit to being impatient through this testing. Help me glean and gather with a right attitude. Help me work steadily, taking short rests and then returning to what You have given me to do. Embolden me to set my own desires aside, to bear witness to the majesty of You, the field owner. Strip away any aspect of my attitude that does not glorify You. Help me to be patient with those with whom I work. Help me in my unbelief and impatience. Teach me to be more like Jesus, whose right attitude never faltered. Teach me that industriousness takes second place to thankfulness, especially in the following area: _____

_____.

REFRESHED AND RENEWED

God wants to see you respond to His loving guidance, correction, encouragement and counsel! Remember, more of God's abundance is given to those who properly take care of what they've already been given. What insights have you sensed God sharing with you today? How might you begin putting them into action?

_____

_____

_____

WEEK 4 - DAY 5

TODAY'S SELECTED BREW: Ecclesiastes 11:10

> *So then, banish anxiety from your heart*
> *and cast off the troubles of your body, for*
> *youth and vigor are meaningless.*

The book of Ecclesiastes is attributed to wise King Solomon. The book's primary aim is to show the emptiness and dissatisfaction that comes from pursuing earthly goals and blessings as ends in themselves. Contrast this with the fullness and satisfaction that come from living a God-honoring life. This scripture points to the attitude of peace and serenity that serves those who are caught in the struggle brought about by earthly anxiety, ill health, and other daily life challenges.

CUPPA INSPIRATION

1. Would you say you experience more anxiety in your personal or professional life?

_____

2. The fact remains that youth and vigor diminish with age. Since there's practically nothing you can do to control this process, is there anything that you *can* control in your personal and professional life?

_____

_____

_____

3. What kind of professional or personal anxieties is God asking you to cast from your heart?

_____

_____

_____

HEAVENLY AROMA

Physician of the Universe, the anxieties of my heart and the troubles of my body have conspired to pull my focus away from You. I confess that I have often stepped off the righteous path, believing that youth and vigor were more important than a relationship with You. Lead me back to You, Lord. Keep me from the preoccupation I sometimes feel about the passage of time. I see my life hurtling toward its natural consequence, and it overwhelms me. Father, I realize that every moment is precious and must be lived with a thankful heart and a right attitude. But sometimes I despair. I see time pass and I am not where I—or others in my life—wanted me to be. I am tired of this battle, Lord. Draw me into Your enfolding arms. Help me achieve the right attitude about Your plan for my life, particularly today as I face: _____

_____

REFRESHED AND RENEWED

God wants to see you respond to His loving guidance, correction, encouragement and counsel! Remember, more of God's abundance is given to those who properly take care of what they've already been given. What insights have you sensed God sharing with you today? How might you begin putting them into action?

_____

_____

_____

Java Break: Attitude

WEEK 4 - DAY 6

COFFEE CAKE, SCONES AND DONUTS

Today, you have the opportunity to reflect over the insights God revealed during the week. In doing so, you'll bake up a treat to share with someone else! Please check the statements that reflect your relationship-building experience over the past few days:

- ☐ I'm learning more about expressing thankfulness.
- ☐ I'm expressing my needs in a way that builds my confidence in God.
- ☐ I'm receiving answers in a variety of ways.
- ☐ I'm experiencing new blessings.
- ☐ I'm involved in a process of change—making character adjustments as God inspires me.
- ☐ I see myself growing in my spiritual walk each day.
- ☐ I'm becoming intentional about building a relationship with God.

This week's *Java Time! with the Lord* focused on suggestions to maintain a Christ-like attitude—both on and off the job. Please reflect, review and restate the insights you've received along the way, as well as the heart attitude changes you have begun to incorporate into your life:

1. What inspirational insights are you seeing that will help you develop a more Christ-like attitude?

_____

_____

_____

2. What heart attitude changes are you making?

_____

_____

_____

3. As you continue to build your relationship with the Lord, where, how or with whom can you share your insights on what it means to develop a more Christ-like attitude?

_____

_____

_____

Ruth's Elixir
Mix 2 cups of milk, 4 tsp. sugar & 4 tsp. of Turkish coffee. Heat these ingredients together on medium heat. Keep stirring! The mixture will boil and foam. Remove from the heat after the foam reaches a couple of inches high. Pour the elixir into small cups and divide the foam evenly. Sip cautiously. The grounds will settle to the bottom of the cup.

Java Break: Consistency

WEEK 5 - DAY 1

Susan's Story

"My son is 15. He wants to go to driver's education to get his license, but I won't let him go.

"For the last 10 years, this child has refused to wear his seat belt. I've calculated that I've had to remind him about 7,200 times over the last decade to put it on. To this day, he refuses to wear the belt without being told to do so, and he gives me all kinds of excuses why he forgot, didn't want to, or didn't think he should have to. I've told him that he is single-handedly responsible for his not getting a license. Period.

"But if I was really honest with myself, I would admit that I have a similar problem. Not with seatbelts, but with exercise. I've been trying to lose weight for years, but no matter how many times I tell myself to do it, I just don't seem to be consistent in my commitment. I have all kinds of excuses why I forget, don't want to, or don't think I should have to. I am single-handedly responsible for my not losing weight. Period.

"One day I told my son that I was finished badgering him about the seatbelt. He knew what the requirements for going to driver's ed were. When he was good and ready, he'd do what needed to be done, and the reward would be a driver's license.

"In the same way, I told myself that I was finished badgering myself about the exercise. I knew what the requirements were for losing weight and getting fit. When I was good and ready, I'd do what needed to be done, and the reward would be a new wardrobe and a better feeling about myself.

"And I began to mature in my faith, too. From that day on, I made the commitment to wake early, to pray, to enroll in a Bible study and stick with it to the end, and to ask God for help in keeping my commitment to the exercise program. I am no longer willing to be the one holding myself back from realizing my full potential.

"My son will also learn this lesson as he sees his mother consistently working toward an important goal."

Ask yourself...
Who's in your driver's seat?

On Being Consistent

Consistency. Some describe it as dependability and reliability. Others say it's about integrity. Still others say it's about follow-through and commitment. How do you define it?

The Bible is full of examples of consistent behavior to achieve a specific outcome. Consider Moses' walking with the Lord despite the overwhelming challenges of the complaining Israelites. Consider Ruth's caring for her bitter, widowed mother-in-law when she could have returned to her own homeland. Consider Christ's moving toward the final mission despite the knowledge of what was to come. Can you say the same about yourself?

What does God tell us about being consistent? That is the focus of the lessons for this week. He wants us to apply ourselves consistently to everything we set out to do. Temporary defeats are expected along the way, but it's the over-all, long-term, forward-looking witness that determines whether we have measured up in His eyes.

Are you a false-start kind of person? Do you begin projects, stop midway, or constantly change direction? Do you find it difficult to follow your tasks through to the end? Do you tend to procrastinate or delegate unpleasant responsibilities to others? Do you make plans and break them at the last minute? Do you suffer from a lack of consistency?

We all can benefit from a change of heart in the area of consistency, reliability, and dependability. As you walk with Christ this week, you'll discover a changed "heart attitude" emerge. At the end of the week, you'll have a new perspective on what it means to be consistent in your personal and professional life. And, most important, you'll acquire valuable tools to help you realize your full potential.

As you proceed through the week's exercises, pay attention to how the Lord begins to partner with you. Watch your relationship with Him blossom as your interaction grows. Experience a new sense of freedom in the way you relate to others. By the end of the week, you'll emerge with a fresh new attitude—one that will bring you closer to the abundance God has for you. As you proceed through the week's exercises and undergo a process of formation into His likeness, be aware of how the Lord partners with you. Ask yourself some questions:

- How is He reaching His desired goal in my life?
- How is He helping me become a real reflection of Him, His nature and ways?
- How have I shown my resemblance to Him in my interaction with others?

Watch your relationship with Him blossom as your interaction grows. Experience a new sense of freedom in the way you relate to Him and to others. By the end of the week, you'll emerge with a fresh new attitude—one that will bring you closer to the fulfillment of God's abundance for you, and hopefully, it will be one that you'll feel encouraged to share!

Java Break: Consistency

WEEK 5 - DAY 2

TODAY'S SELECTED BREW: 1 Kings 11:9-10

> *The Lord became angry with Solomon because His heart had turned away from the Lord, the God of Israel, who had appeared to Him twice. Although he had forbidden Solomon to follow other gods, Solomon did not keep the Lord's command.*

The Book of Kings provides the history of the kings of Israel and Judah from Solomon's ascension to the Babylonian captivity. This passage prophesies the breakdown of the Israelite nation into the two kingdoms—Judah and Israel. This divine chastisement occurred because King Solomon began worshipping his wives' pagan idols.

CUPPA INSPIRATION!

1. Consistency is a behavioral choice. It is linked to dependability, integrity and reliability. Solomon—the wisest man in the world—lost his integrity. Why?

2. As a result of Solomon's willful, purposeful error and lapse in consistency, God punished him. God took away the one thing that mattered the most to the king—his kingdom. Have you ever been in a situation where something you worked hard for was suddenly taken away because you stopped taking care of it? According to that scripture, why might that have happened?

_____

_____

3. God allowed the curse that Solomon received because of his inconsistency to fall on his son. Have you considered that your consistency—or lack of it—may impact future generations?

_____

_____

_____

HEAVENLY AROMA
Ruler of the kings of the earth, I have not consistently acted as though my choices and actions might impact future generations. I confess that I lack commitment in many areas. Lord, teach me to be more consistent in wanting to know You. Guard me from spiritual coldness. Wake me early, Lord. Help me make room in my day for quiet time with You. Build in me a hunger for the Word, the true bread of life. Create in me a desire to consistently reach for You in the face of personal and professional trials, rather than relying on my own strength. I ask for your guidance today, as I face:

_____ .

REFRESHED AND RENEWED
Remember, more of God's abundance is given to those who properly take care of what they've already been given. God wants to see you respond to His loving guidance, correction, encouragement, and counsel! What insights have you sensed God sharing with you today? How might you begin putting them into action?

_____

_____

_____

Java Break: Consistency

WEEK 5 - DAY 3

TODAY'S SELECTED BREW: Psalms 33:11

> *But the plans of the Lord stand firm forever, the purposes of His heart through all generations.*

The Book of Psalms—passionate hymns, songs, anthems, and lamentations—was originally meant to be sung along with a musical accompaniment. Each psalm represents the Israelites' yearnings before God.

CUPPA INSPIRATION

1. The Lord's plans and purposes stand firm forever. He is a consistent, reliable, and dependable God whose character is unshakable and unchangeable. He does not alter His plans midstream. Nor is He manipulated by the whims of others. Are you a woman after God's own heart?

_____

2. When business slumps, there's a tendency to quickly change plans—perhaps even try new approaches, fads, ideas, etc. What are the dangers involved with this approach?

_____

_____

3. If consistency means doing your best each day and not giving in to the temptation to slack off or operate in spurts, how would you rate your performance both at work and in your personal life? How could you be better?

_____

_____

_____

HEAVENLY AROMA

Lord, Refiner and Purifier, why do I sometimes falter, Lord, when things get tough? Why do I change plans midstream and back out of commitments that no longer appeal to my material self? Lord, I am guilty of inconsistency in many aspects of my life. My choices, my desires, my diet, my daily commitments, my work ethic, my faith. Help me get back on track, Lord, with God-honoring decisions that bring me in line with Your plans and purposes. Outside of your grace and guidance, I might never achieve my potential. I ask for that extra measure of courage to stay on the straight and narrow, to purposefully maintain my direction until You direct me otherwise. Keep me from being fickle in my approach to responsibility. Protect me from the world's inconsistency, the unreliable, and the faddish, for these things will not prevail in the end. Help me especially be consistent in: _____

_____.

REFRESHED AND RENEWED

What insights have you sensed God sharing with you today? How might you begin putting them into action? God wants to see you respond to His loving guidance, correction, encouragement and counsel! Remember, more of His abundance is given to those who properly take care of what they've already been given.

_____

_____

_____

Java Break: Consistency

WEEK 5 - DAY 4

TODAY'S SELECTED BREW: Acts 6:3-4

> *Brothers, choose seven men from among you who are known to be full of the Spirit and wisdom. We will turn this responsibility over to them and will give our attention to prayer and the ministry of the word.*

Acts 6 addresses the complaint of the new Greek Christians, whose widows, according to tradition, were to be cared for by the church. To remedy the fact that they were not being ministered to, the apostles delegated the responsibility to the church deacons—Spirit-filled men of good reputation. In this way, the apostles would be free to devote themselves to their calling—consistently praying, preaching and teaching the Word—leaving the day-to-day practical ministry to those who were more gifted in that area.

CUPPA INSPIRATION

1. Are you the kind of person who takes on more than is required of you? Or do you balk or rebel when someone asks you to take on something outside of your main responsibility?

_____

2. When you are asked to do something, do you take time to pray about it or do you just answer yes or no?

_____

_____

3. How can you more consistently invest your talent, skill, ability, and gifts in the workplace? At home? At church?

_____

_____

_____

HEAVENLY AROMA

Father and heavenly Redeemer, through the choices I have made and the circumstances that You have engineered, I find myself at this place and moment in time. What is it that You are preparing me for, Lord? What is it that You want me to learn now? Sometimes I am overwhelmed with what You call me to do. Infuse me with the strength to consistently stay dedicated to the responsibilities You have placed in my charge. Create a barrier against the temptation to give up on something before it has come to fruition in a way that honors You. Bring faithful Christians into my path to help me understand the road on which I am travelling. Help me become more consistent today, as I follow-through with the following responsibility: _____

_____.

REFRESHED AND RENEWED

God wants to see You respond to His loving guidance, correction, encouragement, and counsel! Remember, more of His abundance is given to those who properly take care of what they've already been given. What insights have you sensed God sharing with you today? How might you begin putting them into action?

_____

_____

_____

Java Break: Consistency

WEEK 5 - DAY 5

TODAY'S SELECTED BREW: 1 Chronicles 21:8

> *Then David said to God, "I have sinned greatly by doing this. Now, I beg you, take away the guilt of your servant. I have done a very foolish thing."*

With God's help, King David amassed a huge kingdom that rivaled those of all other kings. Satan took advantage of David's pride and tempted him to take a census of the people in Israel and Judah. God chastened and corrected David for becoming so proud of the sizeable nation over which he ruled.

CUPPA INSPIRATION

1. What are your feelings toward the work you do and the people with whom you work?

_____

_____

2. How do you feel when your accomplishments and hard work go unappreciated?

_____

3. When David accepted the punishment for being proud of his accomplishments, he begged God for mercy, even though he knew he had displeased Him. This pleased God because it displayed his humility. Do you consistently find it difficult to admit when you have made a mistake? Do you consistently give God the glory for your accomplishments?

_____

_____

_____

HEAVENLY AROMA

Great Judge of the Universe, sometimes I find myself over-valuing my contributions. Other times, I find it so hard to admit when I make a mistake. Why are my emotions so touched? Why do I feel I must have an answer for everything? Is it necessary to be right all the time, Lord? Father, I thank you for mercy. For the second and third chance You give me to redeem myself in Your eyes. Remind me that it is okay to fail, but not to be foolish. That it is okay to try, but not to judge. That it is okay to celebrate, but not to idolize. That it is okay to celebrate accomplishment, but not to covet the glory. Create in me a clean spirit, Lord, one in which I can consistently monitor my heart, to come clean before You, and start fresh each and every day. Help me now, Lord, as I try to become more consistent about: _____

_____ .

REFRESHED AND RENEWED

Remember, more of His abundance is given to those who properly take care of what they've already been given. God wants to see you respond to His loving guidance, correction, encouragement and counsel! What insights have you sensed God sharing with you today? How might you begin putting them into action?

_____

_____

_____

Java Break: Consistency

WEEK 5 - DAY 6

COFFEE CAKE, SCONES AND DONUTS

Today, you have the opportunity to reflect over the insights God revealed during the week. In doing so, you'll bake up a treat to share with someone else! Please check the statements that reflect your relationship-building experience over the past few days:

☐ I'm learning more about expressing thankfulness.
☐ I'm expressing my needs in a way that builds my confidence in God.
☐ I'm receiving answers in a variety of ways.
☐ I'm experiencing new blessings.
☐ I'm involved in a process of change—making character adjustments as God inspires me.
☐ I see myself growing in my spiritual walk each day.
☐ I'm becoming intentional about building a relationship with God.

This week's *Java Time with the Lord* focused on suggestions to experience consistency in your life. Please reflect, review and restate the insights you've received along the way, as well as the heart attitude changes you have begun to incorporate into your life:

1. What inspirational insights are you seeing that will help you develop consistency in your relationship with the Lord?

_____
_____
_____

2. What heart attitude changes are you making?

_____
_____
_____

3. As you continue to build your relationship with the Lord, where, how or with whom can you share your insights on what it means to develop consistency?

_____

_____

_____

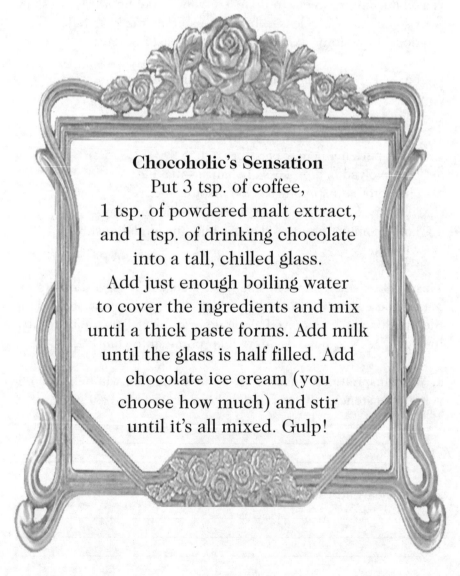

Chocoholic's Sensation
Put 3 tsp. of coffee,
1 tsp. of powdered malt extract,
and 1 tsp. of drinking chocolate
into a tall, chilled glass.
Add just enough boiling water
to cover the ingredients and mix
until a thick paste forms. Add milk
until the glass is half filled. Add
chocolate ice cream (you
choose how much) and stir
until it's all mixed. Gulp!

WEEK 6 - DAY 1

Grace's Story

"My difficult childhood manifested itself in addictive behavior in my teens. By the time I was an adult, I had come down with a debilitating psychological disorder that kept me going from counselor to counselor, taking dozens of medications and generally sleeping my days away, when I wasn't watching TV.

"It was hard to keep a job under these circumstances, so I was eventually put on disability. As such, I was limited to the amount of money I could make, and generally lived at the poverty level in a little house that I rarely kept up. I blamed my situation on my parents, my two ex-husbands, my lazy kids, and whatever else I could find outside of myself. I, of course, was blameless. I was so conditioned to living in my depression that I began to hate life and curse God.

"One day, I was flipping through the TV channels and happened to stop on a Christian station. A woman was looking into the camera and pointing at me! She said, 'Whatever you turn to in your moment of need, THAT IS your god!'

"It took me about two seconds to realize she was talking to me! It was true. In my depression, I had turned to medication, food, sleep, and negativism. The barriers to a normal life—all perceived and none real—had conspired to keep me a prisoner.

"I made a list of every 'idol' I had turned to during the past 30 years. First, there were the prescription drugs I took, thinking they would make me feel better. Then there was the TV. I watched hours of it every day, thinking it was providing entertainment and mental stimulation. Soap opera characters became my friends, as I didn't have any real relationships. Oh, yes, then there was the comfort food. There was plenty of that—never enough, and never quite satisfying unless I gorged. Drugs, TV, and food were the the gods that I turned to in my moments of need. If I had had extra money, I'm sure I would have turned to shopping, too.

"In any case, now I knew the truth. The problem was that I didn't know what to do with what I had just discovered. It would mean I would have to change something—make a decision, get off my duff, try something new. I was sick of living the life I was living. But where to start?

"I turned back to that Christian channel and prayed that there might be an answer there."

Ask yourself...
"What gods do you turn to in YOUR moment of need?

On Breaking Down Barriers

Obstacles, challenges, blocks. Whether perceived or real, barriers can be helpful as well as harmful. The work world is full of barriers—hostile people, difficult situations, baffling problems, discrepancies in compensation. We carry these challenges from home to work, and back again. They become heavy because we lug them to and fro, and eventually they will pull us down unless we learn to unload them at the foot of the Cross.

Barriers can also be helpful and can inspire us to grow. They allow us to exercise faith and obedience. They teach us how to rely on an unseen God who will shoulder those worrisome obstacles so that we might move freely through the world, demonstrating His incredible availability and love for us. Barriers teach us.

Barriers require that we overcome our fear and skepticism before we are broken in half. Barriers are set up to prove God's love for us, and so that we can prove our love for Him.

There are many barriers to success in the work place. For many working women, the barrier is a sense of guilt at having to leave their children in day care. Another barrier is office politics, making it difficult to get work done on time or on budget. For some, a barrier may involve the lack of experience or education required to move up in a company. Barriers are real, but they *can* be overcome.

We all can benefit from a change of heart in the area of overcoming barriers. This changed "heart attitude" will become the focus of your time with the Lord over the next few days. At the end of the week, you will have a new perspective on what it means to break down barriers. And, most important, you will acquire valuable tools to help you realize your full, mature potential.

As you proceed through the week's exercises and undergo a process of formation into His likeness, pay attention to how the Lord partners with you. Ask yourself some questions:

- How is He reaching His desired goal in my life?
- How is He helping me become a real reflection of Him, His nature and ways?

- How have I shown my resemblance to Him in my interaction with others?

Watch your relationship with Him blossom as your interaction grows. Experience a new sense of freedom in the way you relate to Him and to others. By the end of the week, you'll emerge with a fresh new attitude—one that will bring you closer to God's abundance for you, and hopefully, it will be one that you'll feel encouraged to share!

Enjoy your brew!

WEEK 6 - DAY 2

TODAY'S SELECTED BREW: Judges 3:1-4

> *These are the nations the Lord left to test all those Israelites who had not experienced any of the wars in Canaan (he did this only to teach warfare to the descendants of the Israelites who had not had previous battle experience): the five rulers of the Philistines, all the Canaanites, the Sidonians, and the Hivites living in the Lebanon mountains from Mount Baal Hermon to Lebo Hamath. They were left to test the Israelites to see whether they would obey the Lord's commands, which he had given their forefathers through Moses.*

The Israelites were about to enter the Promised Land with its bountiful harvest, rich fields and abundant gifts. After a difficult life in the desert, they were headed toward a life of comparative luxury—a life which would tempt them to become soft, gluttonous, and perhaps even lazy. By creating barriers against which the Israelites would have to test their strength and discipline, God would teach them how to defend what He was giving them. At the same time, He would also see whether His people would obey the commands He had given them, through Moses, in the wilderness.

CUPPA INSPIRATION

1. Are you hoping to arrive at a place in your professional life where you can enjoy a life of comparative luxury? What warning does this scripture give us about such a life? _____

2. God did not bring the Israelites to the brink of the Promised Land just to abandon them. He placed difficult barriers in their path. Why?

_____

3. What is the number one barrier you sense that God has placed in your life? According to the scripture, what is the reason for this challenge?

_____

_____

HEAVENLY AROMA

Lord, You are the Spirit of fire and purification! Thank You for the test as well as the way to remove life's barriers and obstacles from my path. I confess that it is only my unbelief that separates me from You—only the superficial challenges that the enemy uses to keep me from You, especially when he sees my resolve. Help me realize that neither my education, economic status, disability, physical appearance, family background, marital situation, nor ethnic background are true obstacles to becoming all I can be in Christ. Open my eyes to the truth. Help me never to be weary in my walk, as I: _____ .

REFRESHED AND RENEWED

God wants to see you respond to His loving guidance, correction, encouragement and counsel! Remember, more of His abundance is given to those who properly take care of what they've already been given. What insights have you sensed God sharing with you today? How might you begin putting them into action?

_____

_____

WEEK 6 - DAY 3

TODAY'S SELECTED BREW: Judges 6:15

> *"But Lord," Gideon asked, "how can I save Israel? My clan is the weakest in Manasseh, and I am the least in my family."*

Gideon would become the fourth in a line of judges that governed the Israelites after they entered the Promised Land. In this passage, God called Gideon, by way of an angel, to command forces against the warring Midianites. Up to this point, Gideon was known to be active and brave, but he was a relatively unknown figure among leaders. This would change the instant God stepped in.

CUPPA INSPIRATION

1. God promised to give Gideon the strength necessary to overcome opposition on the battlefield. But Gideon only saw his own limitations and the weaknesses of his clan. He did not trust that God could work through him to overcome those barriers. How do you see yourself in light of the barriers in your life?

_____

_____

2. Gideon believed he would have to champion the fight and overcome all barriers by himself, without the resources of the Lord. What phrase indicates this?

_____

_____

_____

3. When confronted with a project that appears to test your capabilities and stretch your competence, how do you feel? Overwhelmed? Overconfident? According to the passage, why are your feelings untrustworthy?

_____

_____

_____

HEAVENLY AROMA

Lord, You who search hearts and minds, thank You for every challenge in my path. I confess that I may not understand when I come face-to-face with Your power. Remind me that it is not I who can win the battles of life, but rather You, working through me. Help me to not feel broken and hurt when things don't go my way. Tug at my heart, Lord, and make me a better, more trusting believer. Continue to test me, then show Yourself strong! Help me in my unbelief. I ask for assistance breaking down the barrier of:

_____ .

REFRESHED AND RENEWED

God wants to see you respond to His loving guidance, correction, encouragement, and counsel. Remember, more of His abundance is given to those who properly take care of what they've already been given. What insights have you sensed God sharing with you today? How might you begin putting them into action?

_____

_____

_____

WEEK 6 - DAY 4

TODAY'S SELECTED BREW: Nehemiah 2:18

> *I also told them about the gracious hand of my God upon me and what the king had said to me. They replied, "Let us start rebuilding." So they began this good work.*

Nehemiah was the king's cup bearer—the one who drank first from the king's cup in case it had been poisoned. Nehemiah had a vision to rebuild the walls of Jerusalem after the Babylonians destroyed them. Pleading his case before his benevolent master—King Cyrus—Nehemiah was given permission to return to Jerusalem along with other freed captives. However, this was just the beginning of the challenges Nehemiah would face. How was he going to be able to motivate a broken people to join him in his temple rebuilding campaign?

CUPPA INSPIRATION
1. Read the passage carefully. What words did Nehemiah use to motivate the freed captives to join him in the rebuilding campaign?

_____

_____

2. Nehemiah could have used His position as a court favorite to manipulate the Hebrews into helping him, but he didn't. Rather, he inspired them. What techniques do you use when trying to get people to "buy into" your vision?

_____

_____

_____

3. Has God assigned you a life or work project so big that you can't succeed without His help? What is it and how are you proceeding? How can you be sure of success when you may not have the resources in hand?

_____

_____

_____

HEAVENLY AROMA

Lord, chief Cornerstone, teach me that I can do all things through You! Remind me daily that I should not be terrified or afraid of the challenges You have set before me. Go before me into the wilderness, Lord. Pave a way for me to follow in Your footsteps. Teach me how to see the promise, the vision, and the pathway to the fulfillment of Your plan for my life. Help me keep my focus on You and not on the circumstances and barriers that lie in my way. As You have promised to go before me in the wilderness, roll away every stone that stands as a barrier between us. Help me today, as I break through my unbelief in the area of: _____

_____ .

REFRESHED AND RENEWED

Remember, more of His abundance is given to those who properly take care of what they've already been given. God wants to see you respond to His loving guidance, correction, encouragement and counsel! What insights have you sensed God sharing with you today? How might you begin putting them into action?

_____

_____

_____

WEEK 6 - DAY 5

TODAY'S SELECTED BREW: Isaiah 59:1-2

> *Surely the arm of the Lord is not too short to save, nor His ear too dull to hear. But your iniquities have separated you from your God; your sins have hidden His face from you, so that he will not hear.*

Isaiah, Joel, Amos, and Obadiah were all prophets. In this passage, Isaiah is explaining to those who had been fasting and praying for deliverance why they had not experienced relief from the challenges they faced and the barriers God had placed before them.

CUPPA INSPIRATION

1. Sins separate us from a holy God, but Christ atoned for them through His death, thereby allowing us to come before God, cleansed and purified despite our sin nature. Do you have issues in your past which you feel are barriers that prevent you from coming before God and receiving His blessings or deliverance?

_____

_____

2. When God places people in your life—both believers and non-believers alike—to expose what is in your heart, do you defend yourself or accept the truth even if it hurts?

_____

_____

3. What do you need to do in order to get real with God about re-moving the barriers that stand between you and Him?

_____

_____

_____

HEAVENLY AROMA

Lord, my Counselor, I confess that I am a prisoner of my own sin nature. You have opened my eyes to this truth. Today I relinquish control over my life, and I ask that you cleanse me from all that I have done that has displeased You. You are a holy God, unable to look upon my sin of defiance, self-love, self-confidence, and self-rule. Thank you for the new life that you have given me—a life at the fountain of living water from whose depth I can receive nour-ishment in the face of debilitating thirst. Hear me God, and retrieve me from the pit of my own making. Your arm is long and your ears are keen. I am calling to You from the depths, asking that you break down the barrier and redeem me from the sin of: _____

_____ .

REFRESHED AND RENEWED

What insights have you sensed God sharing with you today? How might you begin putting them into action? God wants to see you re-spond to His loving guidance, correction, encouragement and counsel! Remember, more of the Promised Land is given to those who properly take care of what they've already been given.

_____

_____

_____

WEEK 6 - DAY 6

COFFEE CAKE, SCONES AND DONUTS

Today, you have the opportunity to reflect over the insights God revealed during the week. In doing so, you'll bake up a treat to share with someone else! Please check the statements that reflect your relationship-building experience over the past few days:

- ☐ I'm learning more about expressing thankfulness.
- ☐ I'm expressing my needs in a way that builds my confidence in God.
- ☐ I'm receiving answers in a variety of ways.
- ☐ I'm experiencing new blessings.
- ☐ I'm involved in a process of change—making character adjustments as God inspires me.
- ☐ I see myself growing in my spiritual walk each day.
- ☐ I'm becoming intentional about building a relationship with God.

This week's *Java Time! with the Lord* focused on suggestions to break through barriers both on and off the job. Please reflect, review and restate the insights you've received along the way, as well as the heart attitude changes you have begun to incorporate into your life:

1. What inspirational insights are you seeing that will help you break down barriers?

_____

_____

_____

2. What heart attitude changes are you making?

_____

_____

_____

3. As you continue to build your relationship with the Lord, where, how or with whom can you share your insights on what it means to break through barriers?

_____

_____

_____

Bev's Barrier Blaster
Here's coffee yummy 'nuf to eat!
Combine 8 fl. oz. instant coffee,
8 oz. of butter, 5 oz. sugar, 2 Tbs.
of vanilla extract and add 7 oz. of flour.
Cream everything together and add 10 oz.
of M&M candies or chocolate chips. Roll
walnut-size dough balls. Drop on non-stick
baking tray. Bake for 12-14 min. at 350°
or until edges turn slightly brown.
Cook and munch!

Java Break: Encouragement

WEEK 7 - DAY 1

Leah's Story

"I'll always remember Mrs. Seltzer, bless her soul. Not because she was a good second-grade reading teacher, but because she made such a profoundly negative impact on my life.

"I was always a good reader, even in the second grade. I remember the circle we kids sat in while we took turns reading "Run, Spot, Run." I was so proud of myself. I had worked so hard to be able to read it flawlessly, and I couldn't wait until it was my turn to read. I would be the best reader!

"The anticipation increased as each of us would read a paragraph or two. I sat looking up at the clock. Would there be enough time for me to read? The other kids seemed to struggle with the simple words, but I was ready. I was so excited; I would be the best. How I wanted to impress Mrs. Seltzer. But time was running out and the bell would soon ring.

"Minutes ticked away, and my excitement was mounting as it soon would become my turn to read. Unconsciously, I sat with my hands folded, awaiting my turn. The anticipation was almost too much to bear. My little thumbs began rotating round and round. Teacher would be so proud of me.

"'Leah!' Mrs. Seltzer barked. Every kid in the class stared at me.

"'Stop twiddling your thumbs! Don't you know that only idle people twiddle their thumbs?' she said, believing she was encouraging me to be anything but idle. Idle people? Was I one of them? I supposed so. If Mrs. Seltzer said I was, it must be true.

"The bell rang, and there was no time for me to prove that I was anything but idle. I never did get to read what I had practiced so hard to master. And, during the next 40 years I became a workaholic—trying to compensate for the damage that Mrs. Seltzer had done that day. I needed to prove to everyone that I was anything but idle. Mrs. Seltzer went to her grave never knowing how her encouragement had been received as a curse."

Ask yourself...
Who have YOU encouraged today? Are you sure?

On Being Encouraged

Where does encouragement come from? The Bible is specific about the kind of cheering, feedback, and motivation that is God-honoring. It has everything to do with building each other up, being consistent in supporting others, and making time to be with those who experience challenges. It has to do with faithfully praying for others. It has nothing to do with ourselves, and everything to do with someone else.

It is what the body of Christ experiences when each of us positively interacts with one another. Just as we are all members of the body—each member having a different and unique function—we are all able to reach out and extend a helping word or hand to the next in line.

This is especially important at work. Encouragement in the material world usually comes in the form of a "ding" instead of a helpful word. Women, in particular, are often encouraged to try harder, work longer, and take on more responsibility for less pay—all this in order to make a difference in the life of the organization, in the life of co-workers, and in their own lives.

To be an encourager means having the wisdom to know that you may need to step out of the box and connect with people in a way that you may not have done before. To receive encouragement means to learn grace and humility. Sometimes it's hard to receive a good word, especially when we don't feel worthy. But for those who encourage us, it is a blessing to know that their words are appreciated.

It is commonly known that for every critical comment we receive, it takes nine affirming encouragements to even out the negative effects. Use your daily conversations as a mutual interaction session in which you exchange advice and assurance, encouragement, and positive affirmation to help each other deal with routine problems and stress.

Encouragement in the workplace means many different things. It refers to the relationship we have with our co-workers. It means forgiving our supervisors when they don't acknowledge something we've worked hard to complete. It means listening to others who have been in our shoes and taking their suggestions as advice and not criticism.

Encourage each other with words and deeds. Allow God to guide you in wisdom so that you will know what each person in your life needs to receive in the way of encouragement. Then watch the blessings flow in!

Java Break: Encouragement

WEEK 7 - DAY 2

TODAY'S SELECTED BREW: 1 Peter 2:9-10

> *But you are a chosen people, a royal priesthood, a holy nation, a people belonging to God, that you may declare the praises of Him who called you out of darkness into His wonderful light. Once you were not a people, but now you are the people of God; once you had not received mercy, but now you have received mercy.*

The new believers struggled during the political tyranny of Roman Emperor Nero. The difficulties of building the faith were magnified in the face of imprisonment and death. Feeling as if their contributions were totally unappreciated, they rallied after having received this written encouragement from Peter.

CUPPA INSPIRATION

1. Peter gave the new believers encouragement by reminding them of their special status in God's eyes. Find four examples from the passage that support this.

_____

_____

_____

2. Sometimes the challenges of the workplace make us feel that our efforts go unappreciated. How does this scripture encourage the hard-working woman who feels unappreciated?

_____

_____

_____

3. In the same way that you need encouragement, there are probably other co-workers who could use some as well. How can you be a source of encouragement for them?

_____

_____

_____

HEAVENLY AROMA

Gracious Leader, benevolent King, You have chosen me as one of Your own, a member of the royal priesthood, a member of a holy nation, a people belonging to You. I declare Your praises, for without You, I would still languish in the darkness where hurt and sorrow and frustration would accompany me all the days of my life. What encouragement do I need, Lord, other than the fact that You have given Your all for me. You are my protection and shield, the One who gives me the strength, encouragement, direction, and confidence to make it through the challenges of each day. Encourage me, Father. Let me know that I am on the right track, as I move toward my goal of: _____

_____ .

REFRESHED AND RENEWED

God wants to see you respond to His loving guidance, correction, encouragement and counsel! Remember, more of His abundance is given to those who properly take care of what they've already been given. What insights have you sensed God sharing with you today? How might you begin putting them into action?

_____

_____

_____

Java Break: Encouragement

WEEK 7 - DAY 3

TODAY'S SELECTED BREW: 1 Thessalonians 5:11-15

> *Therefore encourage one another and build each other up, just as in fact you are doing. Now we ask you, brothers, to respect those who work hard among you, who are over you in the Lord and who admonish you. Hold them in the highest regard in love because of their work. Live in peace with each other. And we urge you, brothers, warn those who are idle, encourage the timid, help the weak, be patient with everyone. Make sure that nobody pays back wrong for wrong, but always try to be kind to each other and to everyone else.*

This is the first of Paul's many epistles. It was written about 51 A.D. to the new believers in Thessalonica. It expresses thankfulness and encouragement, particularly in the areas of faith, hope and love. The major theme of this scripture is how we should work and live together in a community of faith.

 CUPPA INSPIRATION
1. This scripture addresses the need to be sensitive to the needs of others around us. According to the passage, what are the seven ways in which we are to encourage one another?

_____

_____

_____

2. Which of the seven are supported in your workplace?

_____

_____

_____

3. How can you implement this model of encouragement in your professional and personal life, even if the material world does not value it?

_____

_____

_____

HEAVENLY AROMA

Lord of Lords, thank You for the truth of encouragement. I ask You to give me patience in the light of my daily challenges. Help me to respect others who work hard, who may be in positions of authority over me, who can mentor, guide, and admonish me. I ask You to help me live in peace with others. Give me the strength to keep me from being timid and weak in the face of daily challenges. Give me wisdom to apply patience and guard me from paying back wrong for wrong. Help me to always be kind to those who cross my path and to become a source of encouragement for those with whom I work, specifically: _____ .

REFRESHED AND RENEWED

Remember, more of His abundance is given to those who properly take care of what they've already been given. God wants to see you respond to His loving guidance, correction, encouragement and counsel! What insights have you sensed God sharing with you today? How might you begin putting them into action?

_____

_____

_____

WEEK 7 - DAY 4

TODAY'S SELECTED BREW: 2 Timothy 1:3

*I thank God, whom I serve, as my forefathers
did, with a clear conscience, as night and day
I constantly remember you in my prayers.*

Many agree that this passage is from Paul's final letter to Timothy. It was written from prison before Paul's death, and we can tell from the tone of the letter that Timothy was like a beloved son to him. In this passage, he reminds Timothy that the best we can do is to constantly pray for others—especially those we love. In our so doing, God will be glorified and our friends encouraged.

CUPPA INSPIRATION

1. Paul was much older than Timothy when this letter was written. In a sense, he was a mentor as well as encourager. Do you have a mentor in your professional life? Do you want one? Could you become one?

2. In today's mobile society, families are often separated from each other by distance and time. That is why it is important to form new relationships with older and wiser encouragers who are also believers. Where do you go to find these encouragers?

3. Who do you know that could benefit from your guidance, en-

couragement, and friendship? Have you approached them with your offer? Why or why not?

_____

_____

_____

HEAVENLY AROMA

King of Encouragement, why do I find it so hard to ask for encouragement from my co-workers and others with whom I come into contact? And why is it so hard to give encouragement to those in need? Lord, what keeps me from reaching out to others? Am I ashamed, fearing that others will see me as weak and incapable? Why is it that I enjoy lending a helping hand but praying for that person seems so difficult? Is it because I do not feel worthy to enter into Your presence with my requests? Do I fear that You will not hear me, or that You are not there? Help me in my disbelief, Lord. I want to come before You with a clear conscience, an open hand, and a willing heart. I want to come before You with my praises and prayers, knowing that You hear them all. I ask that You hear my prayers for my co-workers, particularly in the area of: _____

_____ .

REFRESHED AND RENEWED

What insights have you sensed God sharing with you today? How might you begin putting them into action? God wants to see you respond to His loving guidance, correction, encouragement and counsel! Remember, more of His abundance is given to those who properly take care of what they've already been given.

_____

_____

_____

WEEK 7 - DAY 5

TODAY'S SELECTED BREW: Acts 14:21-22

> *They preached the good news in that city and won a large number of disciples. Then they returned to Lystra, Iconium and Antioch, strengthening the disciples and encouraging them to remain true to the faith. "We must go through many hardships to enter the kingdom of God," they said.*

This scripture is about the hardships Paul and Barnabas faced in the communities in which they spread the Gospel. After having been threatened and physically attacked in all the cities where they went—even to the point of being stoned and left for dead—they kept on encouraging the new believers in their new faith. Isn't it amazing that the welfare of the new churches was more important to them than their own safety?

CUPPA INSPIRATION

1. What was the encouragement that Paul gave to the new believers? Why were these words an encouragement to those who were suffering?

_____

_____

2. When things get hard on the job, who do you discuss it with first? Your boss? Your co-workers? Your spouse? A close friend? What does God want you to do?

_____

_____

3. What questions do you think God wants you to ask yourself before you deal with an on-the-job challenge?

_____

_____

_____

HEAVENLY AROMA

God, mighty Rock, You know what is in my heart every time I face a challenge on the job. The world teaches us to either put up with the hardship or flee. It does not encourage me to turn to You, Lord, and that is exactly what I want to learn to do. I confess that I need Your encouragement and help to stay focused and calm during the winds of change. But like the disciples who needed strengthening, I also need to receive encouragement to remain true to my faith in You. Help me be patient when going through hardships—both on the job and in my personal life. Help me realize my potential in You, Lord, especially as I seek Your guidance and encouragement today in the area of: _____

_____ .

REFRESHED AND RENEWED

God wants to see you respond to His loving guidance, correction, encouragement and counsel! Remember, more of His abundance is given to those who properly take care of what they've already been given. What insights have you sensed God sharing with you today? How might you begin putting them into action?

_____

_____

_____

WEEK 7 - DAY 6

COFFEE CAKE, SCONES AND DONUTS

Today, you have the opportunity to reflect over the insights God revealed during the week. In doing so, you'll bake up a treat to share with someone else! Please check the statements that reflect your relationship-building experience over the past few days:

☐ I'm learning more about expressing thankfulness.
☐ I'm expressing my needs in a way that builds my confidence in God.
☐ I'm receiving answers in a variety of ways.
☐ I'm experiencing new blessings.
☐ I'm involved in a process of change—making character adjustments as God inspires me.
☐ I see myself growing in my spiritual walk each day.
☐ I'm becoming intentional about building a relationship with God.

This week's *Java Time with the Lord* focused on encouragement. Please reflect, review and restate the insights you've received along the way, as well as the heart attitude changes you have begun to incorporate into your life:

1. What inspirational insights are you seeing that will help you be encouraged?

_____

_____

_____

2. What heart attitude changes are you making?

_____

3. As you continue to build your relationship with the Lord, where, how or with whom can you share your insights on what it means to encourage and be encouraged?

COOL QUICKIE
Pour hot coffee into a large glass filled with lots of ice. Add splash or two (or three!) of flavored non-dairy creamer and 1 Tbs. of instant hot chocolate mix.
Mmmm...

WEEK 8 - DAY 1

Deborah's Story

"When the Barnum and Bailey circus came to town, I took the day off from work and spent it with my seven-year-old, Renner. We bulked up on popcorn and drinks and made our way to the center section down front. They were great seats.

"About midway through the first act, he asked me when the lions would come out. He was so excited. He didn't care about the trapeze artists, the elephants, or anything else. He just wanted to see the lions.

"The lion act finally came on. One by one, the lions were led into the arena, and Renner started to squeal in delight. The trainer cracked his whip, and the lions responded by climbing atop their perches, roaring all the while. It was pretty neat, and if I had been seven years old, I would have been mesmerized and thrilled, too.

"But suddenly, one of the lions began to aggressively reach for the trainer with its paw. It jumped off the perch, and the trainer cracked his whip to get him back in line, but the lion wasn't interested in following directions. He was off on his own program. The lion trainer had a difficult chore ahead of him. If the other lions started to follow suit, he'd have a mutiny on his hands. As the trainer cracked his whip, Renner started to cry, thinking that the man was hurting the animals.

"I thought about it for awhile. It occurred to me that without that lion tamer and his whip, the scenario would turn from an entertaining day at the circus to a bloody mess. How like untamed lions we are! If given an inch, we would rush back to our own nature—wild, rebellious and sinful. But instead of a whip, God uses the gentle yet convicting voice of the Holy Spirit who points us in the right direction whenever we're predisposed to return to our own wild nature.

"I explained to Renner that the trainer was not whipping the animals, but rather snapping at the air. The sound of the crack was what the lions needed to follow the trainer's direction. God, on the other hand, uses a small, still voice to lead His children back to Him.

Ask yourself...
When was the last time you heard the crack?

On Seeking Direction

Direction. It means purpose, goal, objective, and plan. It's what we want and what we seek.

Decisions, decisions...there are a million to make each day. Each decision takes us in a different direction, so where do you look for answers? Consider your last major decision. What exactly were the steps you took toward making it? Where did you go for guidance? Hollywood? Madison Avenue? Wall Street? The White House? The Bible?

God's purposes, goals, and directions for our lives don't always jibe with our own. Caught in a temporal life with a predetermined beginning and end, we tend to want the shortest path to the end result. But in God's eternal perspective on time, He may want to protect us from certain discouragement regarding the direction He is leading us. That's when we are to exercise patience. But do we?

Everywhere we turn, something competes for our attention and challenges our decision regarding health, life, beauty, family values, and the use of our money. It's easy to lose our way in light of popular culture and its "me" oriented values, and fall into step with temptation and sin.

When we sin, we have followed the wrong direction. Repentance is necessary to get us back on track, but it is a *process*, not a one-time event. It involves three actions: First, acknowledging that we're lost. Next, assuming personal responsibility for our spiritual failure. Third, by willingly changing our direction in life—from our way to God's way—to get back on track.

If we humble ourselves, God will guide us in the right "way," i.e., the way that leads to life. As we seek that guidance and direction, Jesus will reveal His plan for us in new and marvelous ways.

Yielding to God's direction in the workplace means many things. It means being open to God's will regarding the compromises one must make to balance family and career. It means being realistic—and not discouraged—about whether a climb up the career ladder is in the individual's or family's best interest. It means yielding to God's will when faced with a career change or geographical move.

We all can benefit from a change of heart in the area of direction. As you walk with Christ this week, you'll discover a changed "heart attitude" will emerge. At the end of the week, you will have a new perspective on what it means to seek His direction. And, most important, you will acquire valuable tools to help you realize your full potential.

WEEK 8 - DAY 2

TODAY'S SELECTED BREW: Psalms 25:8-9

> *Good and upright is the Lord;*
> *therefore he instructs sinners in His ways.*
> *He guides the humble in what is right*
> *and teaches them His way.*

The Book of Psalms is divided into five sections, each paralleling the five original books of the Law of Moses. There are many different authors of the Psalms, and scholars agree that they were written at various periods in Israel's history. This Psalm is attributed to King David. In it, he stands on the promise that God will instruct and direct those who ask to be led. To get this direction, one only needs to ask God to reveal Himself through the Spirit and Word. We then choose whether or not to follow the Way once it is revealed.

CUPPA INSPIRATION

1. Do you sometimes question whether you are doing what God wants you to do with your life?

_____

2. Has it ever occurred to you that God wants to walk with you, regardless of the path you have chosen?

_____

_____

3. What does this truth tell you about God's nature and your choices?

_____

_____

_____

HEAVENLY AROMA

Lord, You are the Way, the Truth and the Life. You have revealed Yourself to mankind through the ages. This revelation has more meaning to me than ever before. I am learning how to see You in Your many manifestations—through others, through the Word, through the Spirit, through my circumstances. Thank you for the direction You give me each day when I come before You. I confess that it has been difficult for me to come in humility. I am bombarded with choices each and every day. Everywhere I look, I see the temptation and motivation to make decisions that do not honor You—decisions about my job, family, my material possessions, and my wealth. Sometimes I just don't know where to begin. Teach me to trust You first, especially as I seek direction today concerning:

_____ .

REFRESHED AND RENEWED

Remember, more of His abundance is given to those who properly take care of what they've already been given. God wants to see you respond to His loving guidance, correction, encouragement and counsel! What insights have you sensed God sharing with you today? How might you begin putting them into action?

_____

_____

_____

WEEK 8 - DAY 3

TODAY'S SELECTED BREW: John 12:14-16

Jesus found a young donkey and sat upon it, as it is written, "Do not be afraid, O Daughter of Zion; see, your king is coming, seated on a donkey's colt." At first His disciples did not understand all this. Only after Jesus was glorified did they realize that these things had been written about Him and that they had done these things to Him.

The Apostle John was an eyewitness to Christ's ministry, miracles, crucifixion, resurrection, and ascension. This passage explains that it took Christ's death and ascension to make the disciples finally understand the truth of God's plan of salvation as it was prophesied in the Old Testament.

CUPPA INSPIRATION

1. It is said that hindsight is much clearer than foresight. In this scripture, the disciples referred back to the Old Testament in order to finally understand what had happened to their beloved Leader. This meant examining the past to understand the present. Have you done this in your own life? When?

_____

_____

2. You are where you are in your life because of certain decisions

you made along the way. Can you cite a defining moment when you turned toward God?

———————————————————————————
———————————————————————————
———————————————————————————

3. You cannot relive your life, but you can live a God-honoring one. How will you start?

———————————————————————————
———————————————————————————
———————————————————————————

HEAVENLY AROMA

Lord, You are the One who saves. Thank You for the wisdom and revelation of prophecy. I admit that I am slow to understand all that I hear and read. I am so busy with my day-to-day responsibilities that I forget that I need to have a longer, broader, more spiritual view of life. I want to be led in the right direction. I am tired of forging ahead on my own, only to end up frustrated and misunderstood. As I mature, I understand that the wisdom of the world is not what it is made out to be. Help me appreciate the wisdom of the ages, Father. Fill me with desire for the truth, as concealed in the Old Testament, and as revealed in the New. Help me understand:

———————————————————————————.

REFRESHED AND RENEWED

What insights have you sensed God sharing with you today? How might you begin putting them into action? God wants to see you respond to His loving guidance, correction, encouragement and counsel! Remember, more of His abundance is given to those who properly take care of what they've already been given.

———————————————————————————
———————————————————————————
———————————————————————————

Java Break: Direction

WEEK 8 - DAY 4

TODAY'S SELECTED BREW: Matthew 2:9-12

> *After they had heard the king, they went*
> *on their way, and the star they had seen in the*
> *east went ahead of them until it stopped*
> *over the place where the child was.*
> *When they saw the star, they were overjoyed.*
> *On coming to the house, they saw the child*
> *with His mother Mary, and they bowed*
> *down and worshiped Him. Then they opened*
> *their treasures and presented Him with gifts*
> *of gold and of incense and of myrrh.*
> *And having been warned in a dream not to go*
> *back to Herod, they returned to their*
> *country by another route.*

This passage recounts the sacred journey of the three wise men, following the "directional signals" God used to lead them to the Messiah. When it was time to return to their country, they could have returned via the same route. However, they responded to God's revelation in the dream that had warned them to return home by another route.

CUPPA INSPIRATION

1. In this passage, God guided those who were disposed to find Him. When did you last receive a sign from God that you were on the right/wrong track?

_____

_____

2. When you bring a question to God, do you ask Him to reveal His direction to you in such a way that you can easily understand it?

_____

_____

3. It is well known that God provides direction through Scripture, prayer, circumstance, the Church and others (both believers and non-believers alike). In what way are you most attuned to receiving God's direction?

_____

_____

_____

HEAVENLY AROMA

Lord who provides, thank You for Your divine direction. Teach me to be more sensitive to your spiritual guidance, more attuned to my circumstances, more willing to hear Your voice through the prompting of the Holy Spirit, more willing to listen to the encouragement of others, and more open to receiving the revelation of the Word. I know I need to take time to consult with You before forging ahead. My life has become complex, Lord, and I need Your direction. Help me adjust the way I make decisions to be more pleasing to You. Instill in me a responsiveness and obedience to what my soul knows is right. Help me with: _____

_____ .

REFRESHED AND RENEWED!

God wants to see you respond to His loving guidance, correction, encouragement and counsel! Remember, more of His abundance is given to those who properly take care of what they've already been given. What insights have you sensed God sharing with you today? How might you begin putting them into action?

_____

_____

Java Break: Direction

WEEK 8 - DAY 5

TODAY'S SELECTED BREW: Numbers 9:18-19

> *At the Lord's command the Israelites set out, and at His command they encamped. As long as the cloud stayed over the tabernacle, they remained in camp. When the cloud remained over the tabernacle a long time, the Israelites obeyed the Lord's order and did not set out.*

The book of Numbers deals with laws, regulations, and the experiences of the Israelites in the wilderness. In this section of scripture, the Israelites are being taught how to function within a religious, civil, and military economy in preparation for the challenging events to come. Here we are shown that God guides and directs His people through signs and signals.

CUPPA INSPIRATION

1. The Israelites were able to discern God's direction because they recognized His presence in the cloud and the pillar of fire. How do you recognize God's presence in your life?

_____

_____

2. Sometimes a direction comes from the enemy himself. How would you know the difference?

_____

_____

3. The Israelites were in a constant state of uncertainty about when the cloud would move, and they had to be in a constant state of readiness to march on short warning. How do you keep yourself in a constant state of spiritual readiness in response to God's leading?

_____

_____

_____

HEAVENLY AROMA

Jesus, my Banner, thank You for marching on ahead, clearing the way of enemy forces, and readying the camp for rest. Thank You for traveling this challenging road with me. Whether I am at work or at home, I need the direction that only You can provide. I ask that You confirm Your will in the way that I am most able to receive it. And Lord, I desire to act in a way that honors You, no matter what I am doing. This is my commitment to You. Whether I stay in my present circumstances, or for how long, is up to You. My times are in Your hands. Tell me what You desire me to do and I will follow. I ask for clarification in the following matter: _____

_____

REFRESHED AND RENEWED

Remember, more of His abundance is given to those who properly take care of what they've already been given. God wants to see you respond to His loving guidance, correction, encouragement and counsel! What insights have you sensed God sharing with you today? How might you begin putting them into action?

_____

_____

_____

WEEK 8 - DAY 6

COFFEE CAKE, SCONES AND DONUTS!

Today, you have the opportunity to reflect over the insights God revealed during the week. In doing so, you'll bake up a treat to share with someone else! Please check the statements that reflect your relationship-building experience over the past few days:

- ☐ I'm learning more about expressing thankfulness.
- ☐ I'm expressing my needs in a way that builds my confidence in God.
- ☐ I'm receiving answers in a variety of ways.
- ☐ I'm experiencing new blessings.
- ☐ I'm involved in a process of change—making character adjustments as God inspires me.
- ☐ I see myself growing in my spiritual walk each day.
- ☐ I'm becoming intentional about building a relationship with God.

This week's *Java Time with the Lord* focused on direction. Please reflect, review and restate the insights you've received along the way, as well as the heart attitude changes you have begun to incorporate into your life:

1. What inspirational insights are you seeing that will help you stay focused?

_____

_____

_____

2. What heart attitude changes are you making?

_____

3. As you continue to build your relationship with the Lord, where, how or with whom can you share your insights on direction.

COFFEE SMOOTHIE

Blend 1/2 pint extra strong cold coffee with 1 scoop of vanilla ice cream. Pour over cracked ice and service with a straw. Makes one drink, so consider doubling the recipe if you have a buddy to share it with!

Java Break: Confidence

WEEK 9 - DAY 1

Claire's Story

"I was running late to an office meeting where I was supposed to give a presentation to the new manager of training. It was my big chance to shine, but as luck would have it, my four-year old refused to cooperate that morning.

"On the way to the day-care center I realized I had forgotten my baby's blue blankie. There was absolutely no time to go back and get it. The baby had no idea it wasn't in the car, because she sat in the car seat, totally absorbed with a crunchy Zwieback.

"When we got to the day-care center my daughter figured out that her blue blankie was missing and began to scream. Her tears ran down her cheeks and onto my silk blouse. She wanted her blankie—that soothing object that brought her confidence.

"There was no way I was going to be able to solve this problem gracefully. I was so behind that I had to call in to the office and let them know I would be late. I felt awful, leaving a screaming four-year-old at the day care center with no blue blankie. How could I leave her without something tangible to bring her security?

"I jumped in the car and went on. She wasn't dying, I rationalized, and I didn't like the fact that she had conferred so much confidence onto that stupid blanket. Enough was enough. She was four years old, and I was ready for her to quit dragging that thing around.

"I arrived at the office just as the meeting was starting. I stood up in front of everyone—my new manager included—with bright tear stains on my new silk blouse. At that moment, I felt totally unprepared, with absolutely no confidence to carry me through the rest of the presentation. I asked to be excused for a moment and rushed into the ladies room. There, I said a quick prayer. 'Lord, shelter me with your wings, wrap me in your loving arms, and help me get through this thing.'

"He did. He cloaked me inside a warm blue blankie. Resting in confidence that He would see me through, I returned to the presentation and did what I had to do. I never forgot my daughter's blue blankie again. It was her symbol of confidence and security, as was the prayer I had spoken to God earlier in my frantic day.

Ask yourself...
What do you use for your blue blankie?

On Building Confidence

Confidence. To some, it means the ability to be bold. To others, it means having a sense of assuredness. To most, confidence is something that is built over time. It comes from trying, trying, trying again, and eventually seeing success from your efforts.

The Bible informs us that the source of confidence is God. It is the kind of confidence that grows out of victories in the face of insurmountable odds. It is the antithesis of self-sufficiency. Consider Moses at the Red Sea. There was no self-sufficiency there. If God had not wielded His hand to create a miracle, there would be no story to tell.

Confidence that is instilled in us by God is a gift translated into a personal experience by the Holy Spirit. The Holy Spirit guides, comforts, and helps those who allow it into their life. It is a force that encourages us to move ahead, instilling in us a sense of peace about the decision in front of us—regardless of what the circumstances look like to an outsider.

Confidence from God is a tool that enables us to have a fresh perspective on our day-to-day challenges. Though the challenges may not disappear, they will appear less daunting because we are not going through them alone.

God-given confidence comes in handy in the workplace. It is the force women need to help them accept themselves in a world which values outward appearance over inward character. It is the assuredness that women need to stand up for what's right, despite the gossip. It's the peace that women need when beginning a new job and trying to seek acceptance from their co-workers.

We all can benefit from a change of heart in the area of confidence. This changed "heart attitude" will become the focus of your time with the Lord over the next few days. At the end of the week, you will have a new perspective on what true confidence means. And, most important, you will acquire valuable tools to help you realize your full, mature potential.

As you proceed through the week's exercises, and as you undergo a process of formation into His likeness, pay attention to how the Lord partners with you. Ask yourself some questions:

- How is He reaching His desired goal in my life?
- How is He helping me become a real reflection of Him, His nature and ways?

- How have I shown my resemblance to Him in my interaction with others?

Watch your relationship with Him blossom as your interaction grows. Experience a new sense of freedom in the way you relate to Him and to others. By the end of the week, you'll emerge with a fresh new attitude—one that will bring you closer to God's abundance for you, and hopefully, it will be one that you'll feel encouraged to share!

Enjoy your brew!

WEEK 9 - DAY 2

TODAY'S SELECTED BREW: 1 Corinthians 15:9-10

> *For I am the least of the apostles and do not even deserve to be called an apostle, because I persecuted the church of God. But by the grace of God I am what I am, and His grace to me was not without effect. No, I worked harder than all of them—yet not I, but the grace of God that was with me.*

If you read this too quickly, it appears that Paul is saying that he's better than the rest of the apostles. However, Paul admits to a deep sense of unworthiness compared to them. This may have come from the fact that he did not have a personal experience with the man Jesus as the others did.

CUPPA INSPIRATION:
1. Paul claims deficiency in three areas. Can you identify them?

_____

_____

_____

2. Paul says that by the grace of God, he is what he is. What did God's grace do for a man so full of human deficiency?

_____

_____

_____

3. Compared to others with whom you work, do you feel deficient or confident? Where do those feelings come from?

_____

_____

_____

HEAVENLY AROMA

Lord, my confidence, thank You for Your presence throughout all of life. Eternal Creator, how well You have conceived the earth, the planets, all of nature, and mankind. Your creation swells with wisdom. Everything serves Your purpose. I confess that it is somehow difficult for me to accept that I am a significant part of Your plan. I see myself as deficient in so many ways. Open my spiritual eyes to the truth that I am acceptable to You. Let Christ be my standard for perfection, rather than the model the world sets forth. Give me rest, knowing that I am Your maturing child. Remind me constantly that society's empty solutions only steer me towards self-righteousness and self-pity. It is by Your grace that I am what I am. Help me today, Father, as I live out this truth and: _____

_____ .

REFRESHED AND RENEWED

What insights have you sensed God sharing with you today? How might you begin putting them into action? God wants to see you respond to His loving guidance, correction, encouragement and counsel! Remember, more of His abundance is given to those who properly take care of what they've already been given.

_____

_____

_____

WEEK 9 - DAY 3

TODAY'S SELECTED BREW—Ezekiel 28:3-7

Are you wiser than Daniel? Is no secret hidden from you? By your wisdom and understanding you have gained wealth for yourself and amassed gold and silver in your treasuries. By your great skill in trading you have increased your wealth, and because of your wealth your heart has grown proud. Therefore this is what the Sovereign Lord says: "Because you think you are wise, as wise as a god, I am going to bring foreigners against you, the most ruthless of nations; they will draw their swords against your beauty and wisdom and pierce your shining splendor."

The Book of Ezekiel provides historical as well as prophetic information about the ancient trading city of Tyre—a prosperous, proud, and beautiful city. Though it appeared to the rest of the world that Tyre was a symbol of perfection, God had other plans in mind. Despite its great wealth and reputation, Tyre would be destroyed. No matter how much wisdom, power, and riches the city appeared to have, it was all folly.

CUPPA INSPIRATION

1. The passage refers to the pride, prosperity, and confidence of a city and its people. What have you prayed for those around you who are like that?

_____

2. In this passage, God has cautioned those who were overconfident. What was His warning? Have you seen evidence of this happening in your own life?

_____

_____

3. How can you prove to God that your confidence lies in Him and not in yourself?

_____

_____

HEAVENLY AROMA

Heavenly Father, Ancient of Days, the psalmist sings that among gods there is none like You. No deeds can compare with Yours. You alone are great and do marvelous deeds. I confess that I tend to suffer from worldly confidence and that it often borders on pride. I pray, Father, that You will take this unhealthy drive and infuse me with a desire to strive only toward Christ-likeness, at home and at work. You are my confidence, Lord. From today on, I will give you the glory for all achievement, in Christ's name. I thank you specifically for building my abilities in the following area: _____

_____ .

REFRESHED AND RENEWED

Remember, more of His abundance is given to those who properly take care of what they've already been given. God wants to see you respond to His loving guidance, correction, encouragement and counsel! What insights have you sensed God sharing with you today? How might you begin putting them into action?

_____

_____

Java Break: Confidence

WEEK 9 - DAY 4

TODAY'S SELECTED BREW: Deuteronomy 9:1-3

> *Hear, O Israel. You are now about to cross the Jordan to go in and dispossess nations greater and stronger than you, with large cities that have walls up to the sky. The people are strong and tall—Anakites! You know about them and have heard it said: "Who can stand up against the Anakites?" But be assured today that the Lord your God is the one who goes across ahead of you like a devouring fire. He will destroy them; he will subdue them before you. And you will drive them out and annihilate them quickly, as the Lord has promised you.*

In this passage, the Israelites were about to cross the Jordan and go into battle with stronger nations. Given this bleak scenario, it would have been easy for them to give up before even starting. If they compared themselves to the strong and tall Anakites ("facts"), instead of believing God's promise to destroy, subdue, drive them out and annihilate them ("truth"), they would have lacked the confidence to take the first step and receive their inheritance.

CUPPA INSPIRATION

1. The Israelites found themselves in a predicament: trust God, or rely on the facts at hand. When your

117

confidence is shaken, what do you do?

_____

_____

2. The Lord has promised that if you trust Him, give your life to Him, and serve Him, you will succeed. What do you think that this practically means in your life?

_____

_____

3. Facts versus truth. Given that you have seen God at work throughout the Old and New Testaments, are you in a place in your personal and professional life where you can begin to claim His promise? Why or why not?

_____

_____

_____

HEAVENLY AROMA
Lord, Alpha and Omega, I am ready to step out on faith. I have learned enough about Your nature to want to place my trust in You. I now understand what You want from me: my devotion, my heart, and my life. You want to be the head of my spiritual house, my leader and shield. From today on, Lord, help me trust You more. You have given me direction, opportunity, and freedom of choice. I choose You now, Lord. Beginning here and beginning today, I ask you to uphold me with Your Truth, especially in the area of:

_____ .

REFRESHED AND RENEWED
What insights have you sensed God sharing with you today? How might you begin putting them into action?God wants you to re-spond to His loving guidance, correction, encouragement and counsel. Remember, more of His abundance is given to those who properly take care of what they've already been given.

_____

_____

WEEK 9 - DAY 5

TODAY'S SELECTED BREW—1 Corinthians 2:1-5

> *When I came to you, brothers, I did not come with eloquence or superior wisdom as I proclaimed to you the testimony about God. For I resolved to know nothing while I was with you except Jesus Christ and Him crucified. I came to you in weakness and fear, and with much trembling. My message and my preaching were not with wise and persuasive words, but with a demonstration of the Spirit's power, so that your faith might not rest on men's wisdom, but on God's power.*

Known for sexual immorality and the indiscretions of a material world, Corinth presented a missionary challenge to Paul when he went there to preach in 50 A.D. He lived and worked with a local couple—Aquila and Priscilla—for 18 months, until he was forced out by the local Corinthians, who were not predisposed to hear the truth. However, the Lord encouraged Paul in a vision, which must have given him comfort and confidence.

CUPPA INSPIRATION

1. Paul lived and worked in an environment that challenged his spiritual values. Yet, his confidence in God was never shaken. How did Paul do it?

_____

_____

2. Paul's effectiveness required serious study, preparation, and reliance on the Holy Spirit. He also needed the fellowship of other believers, such as Priscilla and Aquila. Over the last few weeks, how much time have you spent with other believers?

_____

_____

3. Have you received comfort and the building of God-honoring confidence from this *Java Time!* study? How so?

_____

_____

_____

HEAVENLY AROMA

Father, indescribable Gift, I feel more confident about my relationship with You than ever before. I see how You are leading me down pathways of righteousness in the workplace as well as at home. I am so pleased with the direction You are taking me. I know that You are at work in my life in a significant way. Thank you for standing by me, for revealing Yourself to me, and for providing me with the confidence to move forward toward: _____

_____ .

REFRESHED AND RENEWED

God wants to see you respond to His loving guidance, correction, encouragement and counsel! Remember, more of His abundance is given to those who properly take care of what they've already been given. What insights have you sensed God sharing with you today? How might you begin putting them into action?

_____

_____

_____

Java Break: Confidence

WEEK 9 - DAY 6

COFFEE CAKE, SCONES AND DONUTS

Today, you have the opportunity to reflect over the insights God revealed during the week. In doing so, you'll bake up a treat to share with someone else! Please check the statements that reflect your relationship-building experience over the past few days:

- ☐ I'm learning more about expressing thankfulness.
- ☐ I'm expressing my needs in a way that builds my confidence in God.
- ☐ I'm receiving answers in a variety of ways.
- ☐ I'm experiencing new blessings.
- ☐ I'm involved in a process of change—making character adjustments as God inspires me.
- ☐ I see myself growing in my spiritual walk each day.
- ☐ I'm becoming intentional about building a relationship with God.

This week's *Java Time with the Lord* focused on confidence. Please reflect, review and restate the insights you've received along the way, as well as the heart attitude changes you have begun to incorporate into your life:

1. What inspirational insights are you seeing that will help you build confidence?

_____

_____

_____

2. What heart attitude changes are you making?

_____

3. As you continue to build your relationship with the Lord, where, how or with whom can you share your insights on confidence.

_____

_____

_____

Arabica Delight

Add a heaping teaspoon
of ground cinnamon and
1 tsp. vanilla extract into whole
coffee beans before grinding.
Brew enough for 12 cups, but
serve it with warm milk
because it will be
S T R O N G!

Java Break: Circumstances

WEEK 10 - DAY 1

Ellen's Story

"I received a call from the place where I just had a mammogram done. They noticed an abnormality on the films. Could I come in right away? Thirty minutes later, I was in my car headed back to the Women's Imaging Center.

"They showed me the film. There it was, a bright white blob amid a puddle of black tissue. It looked like an insidious cancer, alright.

"They filmed me again. 'You'll know what it is before you leave today,' the nurse said. 'The doctor will be in in a few minutes.'

"I had a peace about me throughout the entire experience. Even driving through traffic, waiting in the waiting room, and flipping through magazines, I didn't feel like a cancer patient. I was calm and quiet and thoughtful of others who, teary-eyed, waiting for their loved ones to come back from biopsy rooms. In my early morning prayer time, I had called my spiritual 911, connected with

God, and asked Him for the provision of a megadose of peace. 'I draw a line in the sand, Lord,' I told Him. 'Beyond this line, help me keep fear at bay!' This gave the Lord the opportunity to prove, once again, that He hears and answers prayer.

"I debated whether or not to call anyone else and decided to keep the doctor appointment a secret until I knew the outcome. But I was not going into the meeting alone. He would be with me. I needed to be alone with Him, to pray, and receive that peace that surpasses all understanding. I directed my thoughts to the mysterious way that God had prepared me for this circumstances. I understood that this was a kind of test.

"Despite the concern, confusion, and ultimate relief when the doctor confirmed that I was cancer-free, I still went through the test of my life with tremendous peace and resilience. The Great Healer was with me each step of my day. This test is behind me, and I know I'll be ready for the next.

Ask yourself...
Is it time to draw a line in the sand?

On Working Through Circumstances

Circumstances. These are situations in which we find ourselves living, working, or relating to others. But to the Christian, a circumstance often carries with it a spiritual lesson, blessing, or challenge.

God creates circumstances in which He is able to reveal something important to us. Whether the situation is difficult or not, it is designed to bring us to a point of realization about who we are in relationship to Him.

Oftentimes, circumstances are difficult or frightening—such as an illness, financial challenge, a relationship issue, or a critical problem with a job. That's when we need to pray, do what we can to deal with the situation, and ultimately trust God for the outcome.

Many times, believers feel that they are exempt from difficult circumstances because they "have God on their side." However, the scripture does not support this belief. In fact, believers and unbelievers alike experience difficult circumstances at times. The difference is that the believer feels confident, whereas the unbeliever has a sense of hopelessness about the situation.

By viewing impossible or difficult situations from God's perspective, we can gain a perspective that is unique to those who believe. A powerful example is young David, as he approached the giant Goliath. In this circumstance, there was no way David could kill the giant. But God came along side him and David was not alone.

God uses circumstances to accomplish His own purposes. Even the most difficult of circumstances can be used by God to train us up in His ways. A struggle is an opportunity to grow, to endure, and to prevail.

We all can benefit from a change of heart in our understanding of circumstances. This changed "heart attitude" will become the focus of your time with the Lord over the next few days. At the end of the week, you will have a new perspective on challenging circumstances. And, most important, you will acquire valuable tools to help you realize your full, mature potential.

Watch your relationship with Him blossom as your interaction grows. Experience a new sense of freedom in the way you relate to Him and to others. By the end of the week, you'll emerge with a fresh new attitude—one that will bring you closer to God's abundance for you, and hopefully, it will be one that you'll feel encouraged to share!

Enjoy your brew!

Java Break: Circumstances

WEEK 10 - DAY 2

TODAY'S SELECTED BREW: James 1:2-5

Consider it pure joy, my brothers, whenever you face trials of many kinds, because you know that the testing of your faith develops perseverance. Perseverance must finish its work so that you may be mature and complete, not lacking anything. If any of you lacks wisdom, he should ask God, who gives generously to all without finding fault, and it will be given to him.

Scholars believe that this letter was written by James—Christ's brother. The new Christians could not believe that there was any divine purpose in their suffering, their loss of job, home, friends and material possessions, despite the fact that this situation was prophesied by Ezekiel (Ezek. 11:16). James reminded them that the enemy was using these circumstances to tempt them away from their new life in Christ. He urges them to remain stable, firm, and principled and reminds them that suffering is intended to improve their character. James recommends that they pray—not for the removal of their affliction—but rather for wisdom to make the best use of it.

CUPPA INSPIRATION
1. Are the circumstances surrounding your career or personal life overwhelming you? In what way?

2. James reminds the believers that the enemy uses circumstances to tempt them away from their new life in Christ. How are you like them?

3. What does James recommend you do when confronted with daunting circumstances?

HEAVENLY AROMA

Lord and Shield, as I enter into the trials of life, I am calmed knowing that You are there with me. I feel peace knowing that the testing of my faith is the seed of perseverance, maturity, and completeness. This life is so transient and brief, Lord. At its end, I do not want to look back and see a work unfinished. You have promised to give generously to those who learn the lessons of life, provided they learn from You. From today on, I will seek the meaning and the wisdom behind every circumstance I face, knowing that You are there in the thick of it alongside me. Give me courage to face: _____

_____ .

REFRESHED AND RENEWED

What insights have you sensed God sharing with you today? How might you begin putting them into action? God wants to see you respond to His loving guidance, correction, encouragement and counsel! Remember, more of His abundance is given to those who properly take care of what they've already been given.

WEEK 10 - DAY 3

TODAY'S SELECTED BREW: Esther 4:14-16

> *"For if you remain silent at this time, relief and deliverance for the Jews will arise from another place, but you and your father's family will perish. And who knows but that you have come to royal position for such a time as this?" Then Esther sent this reply to Mordecai: "Go, gather together all the Jews who are in Susa, and fast for me. Do not eat or drink for three days, night or day. I and my maids will fast as you do. When this is done, I will go to the king, even though it is against the law. And if I perish, I perish."*

The book of Esther was written during the Persian-Greek conflict. Although God's name is not mentioned in this book, His hand is in the circumstances of the conflict that arose between the Jews and Haman, the King's wicked vizier. The story focuses around Esther, a Jewish girl who was brought into the king's harem and who eventually rose to a position of prominence as the queen. When Haman's plan to liquidate the Jews was accepted, it was up to her to come before the King in defense of her people, putting her own life in danger.

CUPPA INSPIRATION

1. After the decree to kill the Jews was given, Esther could have tried to save herself. Or, she could have waited for God to intervene. What did she do?

2. Are you in a position to right a wrong?

3. What did Esther do prior to making a move? What does this suggest to you?

HEAVENLY AROMA

Lord, Protector, have you placed me here, at this specific job, for such a time as this? Is there something I am to do? Something I am to learn? Please reveal Your will to me in such a way that I am clearly convinced. Lord, if it is a wrong to right, then empower me to do so. If it is a helping hand to lend, then show me who I should aid. Like Esther, fill me with the confidence to move forward when others would fall back. Let me not perish, Lord. Help me make the right decision when faced with an awkward, difficult, or uncomfortable truth. Reveal what You would have me do in the following situation: _____

_____ .

REFRESHED AND RENEWED

God wants to see you respond to His loving guidance, correction, encouragement and counsel! Remember, more of His abundance is given to those who properly take care of what they've already been given. What insights have you sensed God sharing with you today? How might you begin putting them into action?

WEEK 10 · DAY 4

TODAY'S SELECTED BREW: Romans 12:1-2

> *Do not conform any longer to the pattern of this world, but be transformed by the re-newing of your mind. Then you will be able to test and approve what God's will is—His good, pleasing and perfect will.*

In this instruction to the Romans, Paul makes a stunning contrast between Old Testament ritual sacrifice and the New Testament of-fering of self as a living, holy and acceptable sacrifice, including one's body and mind and heart. But how? He explains that this sac-rifice of self requires a radical adjustment in lifestyle and mental at-titude. Believers are to stop being ruled by the physical circumstance of their worldly life, including—but not limited to—pride, luxury, vanity, extravagance in dress, and "riotous" living. They are to direct their efforts toward the renewing of their minds, and in doing so, discover God's will for them.

CUPPA INSPIRATION

1. Paul clearly instructs us to resist pressure that would conform us to the worldly circumstances around us. What circumstances are causing you to be weak, impatient, proud, selfish, stubborn, or arrogant?

_____

_____

2. Paul suggests that we should be transformed by the renewing of

our mind. This requires that we turn to the Holy Spirit for redirection and renewal. How would you rate yourself in this area?

_____

_____

3. When was the last time you presented yourself before God as a living sacrifice?

_____

_____

HEAVENLY AROMA

Father of the pure in heart, You have shown me the path of righteousness. You have removed the temptation in my heart to conform to the pattern of this world. I confess that I still need transforming. Renew my mind. Speak to me directly through others, through the Spirit, through the scripture, through music and friendship. Speak to me in such a way that encourages me to present myself as acceptable to You. Test me, Father, and reveal Your good, pleasing, and perfect will. I am ready to follow—even in the workplace—as I know you have my best interest at heart. Help me, Father, as I: _____

_____ .

REFRESHED AND RENEWED

Remember, more of His abundance is given to those who properly take care of what they've already been given. God wants to see you respond to His loving guidance, correction, encouragement and counsel! What insights have you sensed God sharing with you today? How might you begin putting them into action?

_____

_____

_____

WEEK 10 · DAY 5

TODAY'S SELECTED BREW: Joshua 1:5

> *No one will be able to stand up against you all the days of your life. As I was with Moses, so I will be with you; I will never leave you nor forsake you.*

Moses led the Israelites out of bondage, through the wilderness, and into a relationship with God. When he died, Joshua became his successor. Joshua was a military leader who led the Israelites into battle. God promised the Israelites military, as well as spiritual, victory. It is interesting to note that the very name "Joshua"—the Hebrew form of Jesus—means "Jehovah is salvation." The story can also be experienced as a metaphor for the Christian's spiritual journey, conflict, victory, and blessing.

CUPPA INSPIRATION

1. At the death of Moses, Joshua found Himself in an overwhelmingly challenging circumstance. His job required that he finish what Moses had begun—taking possession of the Promised Land. Imagine how he must have felt looking at the task ahead. Do you feel similarly overwhelmed with something you're going through?

_____

_____

2. Every circumstance can be perceived as a challenge or as an adventure. What makes the difference?

_____

_____

_____

3. Every day the working woman faces tough situations, people and temptation. What does the scripture suggest is the best way to conquer these real-life circumstances?

_____

_____

_____

HEAVENLY AROMA

Lord, no one is able to stand up against You. No circumstance is too large for You to reduce to vapor. I confess that I have not always understood or believed this. Sometimes it is too large and incomprehensible for me to accept that You are really there alongside me each and every step of the way. Why do I doubt? Perhaps it is because I have not yet claimed the promise. Lord, You are my shield! Intellectually, I try to move ahead on my own, but spiritually, I understand that without You carrying the standard, there is no way that alone I can reach the promise of the Promised Land. As you were with Moses, be with me. As you were with Joshua, be with me. Change my heart, Father. Change my attitude about my circumstance. Quiet the winds, especially those that seek to: _____

_____ .

REFRESHED AND RENEWED

God wants to see you respond to His loving guidance, correction, encouragement and counsel! Remember, more of His abundance is given to those who properly take care of what they've already been given. What insights have you sensed God sharing with you today? How might you begin putting them into action?

_____

_____

_____

WEEK 10 - DAY 6

COFFEE CAKE, SCONES AND DONUTS

Today, you have the opportunity to reflect over the insights God revealed during the week. In doing so, you'll bake up a treat to share with someone else! Please check the statements that reflect your relationship-building experience over the past few days:

- ☐ I'm learning more about expressing thankfulness.
- ☐ I'm expressing my needs in a way that builds my confidence in God.
- ☐ I'm receiving answers in a variety of ways.
- ☐ I'm experiencing new blessings.
- ☐ I'm involved in a process of change—making character adjustments as God inspires me.
- ☐ I see myself growing in my spiritual walk each day.
- ☐ I'm becoming intentional about building a relationship with God.

This week's *Java Time with the Lord* focused on circumstances. Please reflect, review and restate the insights you've received along the way, as well as the heart attitude changes you have begun to incorporate into your life:

1. What inspirational insights are you seeing that will help you deal with your circumstances?

_____

_____

_____

2. What heart attitude changes are you making?

_____

3. As you continue to build your relationship with the Lord, where, how or with whom can you share your insights on circumstances.

**Quick
Pick-Me-Up!**

Pour 1 cup of coffee,
1 cup carbonated water
and a strip of lemon
over shaved ice.
You go, girl!

Java Break: Commitment

WEEK 11 - DAY 1

Tracy's Story

"One of the most meaningful lessons I ever had about commitment came during the time I was in college. Over the summer break, I traveled to Israel to live with a friend and her family. It was an awesome experience.

"While I was there, I made a commitment to read the Bible cover to cover. I figured since I was in the Holy Land, I ought to learn as much about it as possible. I was a Christian, but not really. It was a head knowledge—and not a heart knowledge—that kept me in church. Mostly, I went because my parents expected it of me.

"But that trip to Israel changed everything. I was able to see the Holy Land from a new perspective, and I hungrily devoured the scriptures.

"One day, we went shopping in the marketplace, and I bought a beautiful gold cross and a chain. I kept it in a little box, nice and shiny, and never put it on. My friend's father asked me why I did this, and I told him it was because I didn't feel I should wear it until I had finished my commitment—reading the Bible cover to cover. I felt I should 'earn' the right to wear the cross.

"He smiled and told me that my approach may seem right to some, but that I should bear the cross and wear it proudly. He said that the Bible is about God and that I can't just read it in order to 'get it.' I needed to expand my commitment to include spending time with Him on a daily basis. That's where the commitment would get harder, because it might mean having to give up some comfort to stick with it.

"I realized that he was right, took the cross out of the box, and wore it proudly since then. A commitment requires a day-to-day approach. It's not an event, but rather a process. I can always read the Bible cover-to-cover, but it's the long-haul decision to come to know the Author that requires the real commitment.

Ask yourself...
Are you bearing your cross and wearing it proudly?

On Keeping Commitments

Commitment. It's a promise or a vow that we make to someone. When God makes a commitment to us, it's called a covenant.

Moses, Abraham, and Christ are just a few of the many individuals throughout history who have made commitments to God, despite the challenges to their safety, comfort, and lives. Though they had to leave their families, friends, and the security of their former lives before making the commitments, they did so knowing it was God's will. Those are the commitments that we must make whole-heartedly.

Most commitments in our society are made with a short-term vision. When things get tough, our commitments fade as if they were never made at all. Consider the commitments that are often made in the work place. In many cases, these commitments are even solidified into contracts, but still broken.

Whenever possible, your commitment should be to God, and not to others. The vow that you make to another person is witnessed by the Lord. That's why your commitments should have a higher calling. If God sees you in everything you do, then you are more likely to keep your commitment.

We all can benefit from a change of heart in the area of commitment. This changed "heart attitude" will become the focus of your time with the Lord over the next few days. At the end of the week, you will have a new perspective on what it means to be effective. And, most important, you will acquire valuable tools to help you realize your full, mature potential.

As you proceed through the week's exercises, as you undergo a process of formation into His likeness, pay attention to how the Lord partners with you. Ask yourself some questions:

- How is He reaching His desired goal in my life?
- How is He helping me become a real reflection of Him, His nature and ways?
- How have I shown my resemblance to Him in my interaction with others?

Watch your relationship with Him blossom as your interaction grows. Experience a new sense of freedom in the way you relate to Him and to others. By the end of the week, you'll emerge with a fresh new attitude—one that will bring you closer to God's abundance for you, and hopefully, it will be one that you'll feel encouraged to share!

Enjoy your brew!

WEEK 11 - DAY 2

TODAY'S SELECTED BREW: 1 Samuel 7:3

*And Samuel said to the whole house
of Israel, "If you are returning to the Lord with
all your hearts, then rid yourselves of the
foreign gods and the Ashtoreths and commit
yourselves to the Lord and serve Him only,
and he will deliver you out of the hand
of the Philistines."*

There was a time in Israel's history when they had no king but instead were directed by judges and prophets such as Samuel. In this passage, the Israelites just lost the sacred Ark of the Covenant (containing the presence of God) to the Philistines in battle. Many were captured and began worshiping local idols. In this dismal scenario, Samuel reminded them that if they would commit to return to God alone—with no excuses, distractions, or second thoughts—then the hazards they faced would not break them. The Israelites did so and were eventually delivered from the Philistines.

CUPPA INSPIRATION

1. Being committed to God means moving ahead faithfully with confidence, regardless of the difficulties, hazards or unknown challenges. Do you live this way or not?

_____

_____

2. What does being committed to God mean with regard to situations in the workplace?

_____

_____

3. When things got tough, the Israelites faltered on their commitment to God, thinking it would make things easier. What do you think would have happened to them in the long term if they had not turned back to Jehovah with a renewed commitment?

_____

_____

_____

HEAVENLY AROMA

Father of Abraham, Isaac and Jacob, thank You for providing me a way to return to You —a way to be at one and at peace with Christ. Thank You for providing a way through the minefields and slick territories that pull me away from my commitments. I confess that I want to serve You with all my heart, but that it has been difficult when confronted with the idols of materialism, self-worship, temptation, addiction, and co-dependence. Today, I recommit myself to You, to turn away from all that glitters and destroys, to seek and serve You only. Forgive me, Father, as I now confess the following:

_____

_____ .

REFRESHED AND RENEWED

God wants to see you respond to His loving guidance, correction, encouragement and counsel! Remember, more of His abundance is given to those who properly take care of what they've already been given. What insights have you sensed God sharing with you today? How might you begin putting them into action?

_____

_____

_____

WEEK II · DAY 3

TODAY'S SELECTED BREW: Joshua 24:14-15

Now fear the Lord and serve Him with all faithfulness. Throw away the gods your fore-fathers worshiped beyond the River and in Egypt, and serve the Lord. But if serving the Lord seems undesirable to you, then choose for yourselves this day whom you will serve, whether the gods your forefathers served be-yond the River, or the gods of the Amorites, in whose land you are living. But as for me and my household, we will serve the Lord.

In a series of magnificent battles led by the Lord, Joshua and the Israelites claim the territory of Israel, killing off all the local clans who worshiped idols. In this passage, Joshua challenges the Israelites to recommit to the Lord Jehovah. As a true leader, he sets the standard.

CUPPA INSPIRATION

1. God expects us to be committed to whatever we have taken on as a responsibility—so long as it honors Him. What commitments have you made that do and do not honor God?

---

2. God has given us the 10 commandments as the starting point of a relationship with Him. What others can you think of?

_____

_____

_____

3. Given that life in the material world encourages us to worship "false idols," do you think it's time to recommit yourself to the Lord?

_____

_____

_____

HEAVENLY AROMA

Lord, Jesus, I come before You with open hands and a broken heart. I come to You just the way I am, a piece of clay waiting to be molded by Your expert, healing touch. Lord, I confess that I need You. Thank You for Your life and Your teaching, for they have opened the path out of the darkness and into the light. Thank You for taking on the burden of my sin, and for dying on the cross so that I might live. Thank You for the mystery of Your resurrection and for the unimaginable glory of Your ascension to the right hand of God. Lord, Jesus. I place my life entirely into Your hands from this day forth. I commit to knowing You more, seeking Your will, and allowing Your cleansing, healing touch in my life. Amen.

REFRESHED AND RENEWED

Remember, more of His abundance is given to those who properly take care of what they've already been given. God wants to see you respond to His loving guidance, correction, encouragement and counsel! What insights have you sensed God sharing with you today? How might you begin putting them into action?

_____

_____

_____

WEEK 11 - DAY 4

TODAY'S SELECTED BREW: Psalms 37:3-4

> *Trust in the Lord and do good;*
> *dwell in the land and enjoy safe pasture.*
> *Delight yourself in the Lord and he will give*
> *you the desires of your heart.*

The theme of Psalm 37 is patience, maturity, and trust. In this verse, David set up a model for success in life, based on the commitments we must make to God.

CUPPA INSPIRATION

1. The scripture sets up a series of formulas for success. Fill in the blank: If you trust in the Lord, you will _____. If you dwell in His land you will _____. If you delight yourself in the Lord, he will_____

2. What does dwelling in God's land mean to you?

_____
_____
_____

3. God will not give you everything you want. He will give you what you need. And as your commitment to Him increases, your wants and needs will begin to align themselves with what God wants to give you. In what ways have you begun to experience this since committing to take this course?

_____

HEAVENLY AROMA

Lord of all Heaven, I am slowly beginning to understand how You work all things together for good in my life. I see Your hand daily in the affairs of my household and my job. I am beginning to experience a sense of connectedness with You that I never thought possible. I ask that You reveal Yourself to me increasingly each and every day. Thank you for the promise of success, safe pasture, and delight. I rest on that promise, and ask that You begin to work in the lives of these others, who I lift to Your throne now:

_____

_____ .

REFRESHED AND RENEWED

What insights have you sensed God sharing with you today? How might you begin putting them into action? God wants to see you respond to His loving guidance, correction, encouragement and counsel! Remember, more of His abundance is given to those who properly take care of what they've already been given.

_____

_____

_____

Java Break: Commitment

WEEK II - DAY 5

TODAY'S SELECTED BREW: 1 Samuel 1:21-22

> *When the man Elkanah went up with all his family to offer the annual sacrifice to the Lord and to fulfill his vow, Hannah did not go. She said to her husband, "After the boy is weaned, I will take him and present him before the Lord, and he will live there always."*

Imagine the character and commitment it would take to agree to dedicate your son to the service of God if the Lord would grant you one desire—to have a child at all. That's what happened to Hannah, who had Samuel after years of praying for a child. When Samuel was weaned, she delivered him to the temple where he would spend his early years being educated among the children of the priests, possibly never to return home again. God honored Hannah's commitment, and Samuel became one of the most well-known prophets of his age.

CUPPA INSPIRATION

1. In this scripture, Hannah kept her promise, even though it cost her the son she always wanted. Has your commitment to God this week cost you something? Or was it just a token gesture to get you through the exercise?

_____

_____

2. In the material world, promises are easily made and broken. Commitment is superficial because it often requires a major change. It would have been easy for Hannah to retract her commitment and keep Samuel at home, but she didn't. Are you a woman of your word in matters of spiritual commitment?

_____

_____

3. God is actually watching to see how you demonstrate your commitment to Him. What have you done to demonstrate to others that you have made this commitment?

_____

_____

_____

HEAVENLY AROMA

Jesus, today I am renewing my commitment to follow You with determination and faith. Like Hannah, I will not turn back. I have brought You my whole self—my head, my hands, and my heart. I keep nothing back, Lord, for You have kept nothing back from me. Hear my petition, Lord, as I ask for Your leading, direction, and blessing in every aspect of my life. Fill me with peace and a sense of security. Reveal Yourself to me in a way that I can see, feel, and hear, especially today, as I ask for: _____

_____.

REFRESHED AND RENEWED

God wants to see you respond to His loving guidance, correction, encouragement and counsel! Remember, more of His abundance is given to those who properly take care of what they've already been given. What insights have you sensed God sharing with you today? How might you begin putting them into action?

_____

_____

_____

Java Break: Commitment

WEEK II - DAY 6

COFFEE CAKE, SCONES AND DONUTS

Today, you have the opportunity to reflect over the insights God revealed during the week. In doing so, you'll bake up a treat to share with someone else! Please check the statements that reflect your relationship-building experience over the past few days:

☐ I'm learning more about expressing thankfulness.
☐ I'm expressing my needs in a way that builds my confidence in God.
☐ I'm receiving answers in a variety of ways.
☐ I'm experiencing new blessings.
☐ I'm involved in a process of change—making character adjustments as God inspires me.
☐ I see myself growing in my spiritual walk each day.
☐ I'm becoming intentional about building a relationship with God.

This week's *Java Time with the Lord* focused on commitment. Please reflect, review and restate the insights you've received along the way, as well as the heart attitude changes you have begun to incorporate into your life:

1. What inspirational insights are you seeing that will help you deal with your circumstances?

_____

_____

_____

2. What heart attitude changes are you making?

_____

3. As you continue to build your relationship with the Lord, where, how or with whom can you share your insights on circumstances.

_____

_____

_____

DIVINE DOLLOP

Need a great topping for
ice cream? Don't throw away
that last cup of thick coffee
in the pot. Add a cup of sugar
and boil it in a saucepan. Let the
concoction simmer for a few
minutes, then refrigerate
for future use!

Java Break: Abundance

WEEK 12 - DAY 1

Christine's Story

"I had lunch with a girlfriend from another company last week. During lunch we caught up on everything that had happened over the past month. We talked about our jobs, families, kids... all the stuff that women usually talk about. At the end of the conversation, we decided to get some dessert. For her, dessert was a bag of M&Ms, and I decided to have cheese cake.

"I confessed to her that I was not sure whether I was going to stick with my career. I felt I had worked very hard, but that I had not prospered the way I thought I would after so many years at it. I confessed that I was worried about finances, and since I was getting older, I was afraid I wouldn't be able to find another good job.

"She asked me some questions and got to the heart of the matter fairly quickly. It wasn't that the business wasn't going well—it was just that I wasn't enjoying it any more. My expectations far exceeded any sense of reality. Although I was, in fact, making a living,

I wasn't "prosperous" because I had let the world's definition of abundance rule my life.

"She poured out the M&Ms on the table and asked me to start counting my blessings. At first, I couldn't come up with any other than my job and my husband. She lined up two M&Ms to represent each of them. Then she started ticking off the blessings in her life, lining up one candy after the other: blessings of a family who loved her, of confidence about the future, of a sense of peace knowing who she was, of friends who cared enough to meet her for lunch, of a safe home to live in, of a full night of sleep, of a caring heart for others, and so many other things that I would never have considered on the first go-round.

"I looked at her row, I looked at mine, and suddenly I understood why I had felt so lacking. The blessings were there, all right. I just chose not to see them. In any case, we started eating the M&Ms, one at a time until we got to the red one.

"I never eat the red one first," she said. "I always save that for last."

"Why do you do that?" I asked curiously.

"That red one reminds me to thank Jesus for bringing me all the rest."

Ask Yourself...
Which M&M do you save for last?

On Redefining Abundance

Abundance. To some it means wealth. To others, it means material possessions. To the Christian, it should mean blessings.

In this age of discontent and greed, finding true abundance seems to be focused on the acquisition of material wealth over spiritual wealth. The "need" to keep up with the Jones' has forced many into debt. The desire to have the best leads many into a sustained season of discontent when they realize that they cannot possibly compete without losing a rational perspective.

The Bible teaches that material blessings are only *one* expression of the love and care that God has for us. But the more wealthy we become, the more likely it is for us to forget God and His role. Material wealth tempts us away from Him and creates in us a sense of independence. This becomes self-reliance, which in turn, becomes self-worship.

What is God's greatest blessing? It is the gift of Jesus. Christ gives life. Without life, there can be no other blessing.

We all can benefit from a change of heart in the area of abundance. This changed "heart attitude" will become the focus of your time with the Lord over the next few days. At the end of the week, you will have a new perspective on what it means to be wealthy. And, most important, you will acquire valuable tools to help you realize your full, mature potential.

As you proceed through the week's exercises, as you undergo a process of formation into His likeness, pay attention to how the Lord partners with you. Ask yourself some questions:

- How is He reaching His desired goal in my life?
- How is He helping me become a real reflection of Him, His nature and ways?
- How have I shown my resemblance to Him in my interaction with others?

Watch your relationship with Him blossom as your interaction grows. Experience a new sense of freedom in the way you relate to Him and to others. By the end of the week, you'll emerge with a fresh new attitude—one that will bring you closer to God's abundance for you, and hopefully, it will be one that you'll feel encouraged to share!

Enjoy your brew!

TODAY'S SELECTED BREW: Luke 12:15

> *Then [Jesus] said to them. "Watch out!*
> *Be on your guard against all kinds of greed;*
> *a man's life does not consist in the abundance*
> *of his possessions."*

In this scripture, Jesus addresses a crowd of many thousands. He warns them to be on guard against the hypocrisy of their spiritual leaders, the Pharisees. He tells them not to be afraid for their physical life, nor for how they will defend themselves before rulers and authorities. Someone in the crowd speaks up, asking Him to speak on the issue of material inheritance, and Christ responds with a warning in the scripture above.

CUPPA INSPIRATION

1. Has there ever been a time in your life when you were worried about your financial state?

_____

_____

2. Have the material concerns of your life—what you wear, the food you eat, the "stuff" you buy—taken precedence over your relationship with Christ in the past? What about now?

_____

_____

_____

3. Having seen how God has worked throughout history in the life

of His people, do you believe that He is trying to teach you something about material wealth through this study? What is it?

_____

_____

_____

HEAVENLY AROMA

Father in Heaven, thank You for the way, the truth and the life. I confess that my life has often been wrapped up in the accumulation of material possessions. My soul reaches toward a higher truth—a meaningful relationship with You. Let me bring this problem to You in prayer, Lord. Show me how I need to change and grow in my understanding of the world's ways. It is You who gives me life—not the material possessions that I have gathered about myself. In You I find abundant forgiveness, love, and guidance. It is in You that I should find my contentment and abundant life. Thank You for providing for my material needs. Please hear my prayer as I ask You to reveal the fullness of Your wisdom as I confront my own issues of:

_____

_____ .

REFRESHED AND RENEWED

God wants to see you respond to His loving guidance, correction, encouragement and counsel! Remember, more of His abundance is given to those who properly take care of what they've already been given. What insights have you sensed God sharing with you today? How might you begin putting them into action?

_____

_____

_____

Java Break: Abundance

WEEK 12 - DAY 3

TODAY'S SELECTED BREW: Mark 10:25

> *It is easier for a camel to go through
> the eye of a needle than for a rich man
> to enter the kingdom of God.*

Jesus used parables and symbols to hold people's attention. In this passage, He reminds us that when our basic physical needs are met—food, housing, companionship, etc.—we tend to become self-reliant and pull back from depending on Him. Sometimes God uses pain and poverty to drive us to Him. When we turn to money to buy something to ease the pain, we are actually creating a deficiency that only God can meet.

CUPPA INSPIRATION

1. Would you say that your basic physical needs are being met now?

_____

_____

2. Do you buy things because others have them? Where do you think that drive comes from?

_____

3. Is the Lord using a financial situation in your life to drive you to Him?

_____

_____

_____

HEAVENLY AROMA

Father of all abundance, I come before You, thankful that You have met my every need. I confess there are times, Lord, when it seems that there will be no solution to tomorrow's financial requirements. In those times, I fall short of the faithful calling to which I aspire—a full and confident belief in You. But if I were honest, Lord, I would see that You have been there for me at each and every crossroad. You have not abandoned me, though I may have turned from You. Lord, why do I doubt? Let it not become a matter of self-sufficiency, Lord, for You are my sufficiency. Fill me with Your peace, Lord, as I struggle today with concerns about: _____

_____

REFRESHED AND RENEWED

Remember, more of His abundance is given to those who properly take care of what they've already been given. God wants to see you respond to His loving guidance, correction, encouragement and counsel! What insights have you sensed God sharing with you today? How might you begin putting them into action?

_____

_____

_____

WEEK 12 - DAY 4

TODAY'S SELECTED BREW: John 10:10

> *The thief comes only to steal and kill*
> *and destroy; I have come that they may have*
> *life, and have it to the full.*

Christ reminds the believer that the abundance He offers is different from that offered by the material world. Physical possessions can be stolen and destroyed, while spiritual blessings—forgiveness, love, guidance—are things that cannot be earned, traded, sold, bought, stored or saved for retirement. They are free for the asking every day.

CUPPA INSPIRATION
1. Have you ever had something stolen or lost? How did you feel knowing you might never see that thing again?

_____

_____

2. It might be argued that in our materialistic society, buying things we don't really need helps keep others in business. What's wrong with this philosophy from a spiritual perspective?

_____

_____

3. Do you think you could get along with fewer "things"? Have you ever tried?

_____

_____

_____

HEAVENLY AROMA

Father and Protector, I understand that it is the enemy's domain to entice me with material things and keep me dissatisfied with what You have already given me. I have a new appreciation of the abundant life, Lord. It stems from a renewed relationship with You. Help me experience the satisfaction of peace, joy, and love. Let me learn to live within my means. Let me tithe back to You what is Yours to begin with, and let me see the magnificent blessings roll in—the result of my faithful commitment. Help me take up arms against the enemy—the thief who has come to rob me of all that You bring into my life. Let me not become so attached to material possessions, Lord, that I forget the source of all provision. It is You. Lord. Help me in my unbelief, especially as I try to: _____

_____ .

REFRESHED AND RENEWED

Remember, more of His abundance is given to those who properly take care of what they've already been given. God wants to see you respond to His loving guidance, correction, encouragement and counsel! What insights have you sensed God sharing with you today? How might you begin putting them into action?

_____

_____

_____

Java Break: Abundance

WEEK 12 - DAY 5

TODAY'S SELECTED BREW: Ecclesiastes 10:19

> *A feast is made for laughter,
> and wine makes life merry, but money
> is the answer for everything.*

Ecclesiastes reminds us that money *appears* to be the answer to every need and every greed. There's a time for everything, Solomon says. The material world offers many unique thrills, but when the thrill wears off we are tempted to want to buy more and more. The passage distinguishes between money that's needed for survival, and the love of money that is the root of all evil.

CUPPA INSPIRATION

1. If you were to suddenly become rich, how would you spend your money?

_____

_____

_____

2. Do you think it's possible to have enough money? Why or why not?

_____

_____

_____

3. We are taught to believe that the money we make belongs to us. But that money was given to us by God to be used to support His plan. In essence, it belongs to Him. Giving God our tithe (10% of

our gross salary) is a tool we use to demonstrate our understanding of this principle. Do you tithe? Why or why not?

_____

_____

_____

HEAVENLY AROMA

Dear Lord, thank You for the lessons of divine abundance. I will no longer lust after the gathering of pennies and dollars—the silver and gold of worldly preoccupation. Instead, I will seek to do Your will, knowing that the provision comes from Your hand and not my own. I will invest my time, talent, and skills into Your Kingdom, for it is there that I plan to spend eternity. I will join with other believers and begin to consistently apply the divine principles that I learn into my professional and personal life. I will test You with the gift of the tithe, expectantly awaiting the incredible blessings that You have promised me if I do. I will appropriate the blessing of the now and the hereafter, Lord, and I will become a shining beacon to others with whom I come in contact. I understand, Lord, that I may be the only face of Christ that many will see. Thank you for giving me purpose, direction, and a future.

REFRESHED AND RENEWED

What insights have you sensed God sharing with you today? How might you begin putting them into action? God wants to see you respond to His loving guidance, correction, encouragement and counsel! Remember, more of His abundance is given to those who properly take care of what they've already been given.

_____

_____

_____

WEEK 12 - DAY 6

COFFEE CAKE, SCONES AND DONUTS

Today, you have the opportunity to reflect over the insights God revealed during the week. In doing so, you'll bake up a treat to share with someone else! Please check the statements that reflect your relationship-building experience over the past few days:

☐ I'm learning more about expressing thankfulness.
☐ I'm expressing my needs in a way that builds my confidence in God.
☐ I'm receiving answers in a variety of ways.
☐ I'm experiencing new blessings.
☐ I'm involved in a process of change—making character adjustments as God guides me.
☐ I see myself growing in my spiritual walk each day.
☐ I'm becoming intentional about building a relationship with God.

This week's *Java Time with the Lord* focused on abundance. Please reflect, review and restate the insights you've received along the way, as well as the heart attitude changes you have begun to incorporate into your life:

1. What inspirational insights are you seeing that will help you deal with abundance concerns?

_____

_____

_____

2. What heart attitude changes are you making?

_____

3. As you continue to build your relationship with the Lord, where, how or with whom can you share your insights on abundance.

Fill It to the Brim!

Take about 4 Tbs. of the coffee syrup from last week's recipe and add 1-1/2 cups (that's ready) of ice cream—your choice of flavor. Add a cup of cold milk and 2 tsp. of chocolate syrup. Blend and eat out of the blender. Saves clean-up!

ABOUT THE AUTHOR

Photography by Tim Scheer

Who would have expected a Jewish girl from Connecticut to champion the cause of Christ in the workplace? But that's what happened when Anne Johns, graduate of SMU and the University of Texas at Austin, heard the voice of God calling to her through a heavy cloud of spiritual darkness.

When challenged by a Christian with the fact that she could no longer solve her own problems, she turned her life over to the Lord. Her years of international corporate experience with such companies as Control Data Corporation, American Airlines, and ARCO International Oil and Gas Company eventually led to a position with an international direct sales organization where she became impassioned with the idea of helping women learn how to balance faith, family, and career. Rising to the position of Senior Sales Director, Anne understood that her gift of teaching would best be served helping working women turn to Christ.

A seasoned public speaker, Anne's ministry reaches into the workplace as well as the home. She is the mother of two children and the supportive wife of David who is in full-time ministry.

To contact Anne Johns for speaking engagements or with comments on *Java Time! for Women,* write or call:

E-mail: Javatime@airmail.net
website: www.javatimebooks.com
888-839-4486 (toll free) • 214-769-4085 (cell)

For information on a *Java Time!* Map to the Treasure Retreat, Expedition, or Bible Study near you, visit www.javatimebooks.com.
